TAKE
THE
HELM

NAVIGATING YOUR WAY
TO FINANCIAL FREEDOM

Roland Ghazal

TAKE
THE
HELM

NAVIGATING YOUR WAY
TO FINANCIAL FREEDOM

Roland Ghazal

Made for Success
PUBLISHING

Made for Success Publishing
P.O. Box 1775 Issaquah, WA 98027
www.MadeForSuccessPublishing.com

Distributed by Made for Success Publishing

Typeset by Nord Compo

First Printing

Library of Congress Cataloging-in-Publication data
Ghazal, Roland
    Take the Helm: Navigating Your Way to Financial Freedom
      p. cm.
LCCN: 2020903459
ISBN: 978-1-64146-495-6 (PPBK)
ISBN: 978-1-64146-495-6 (HDBK)
ISBN: 978-1-64146-496-3 (eBOOK)
ISBN: 978-1-64146-516-8 (AUDIO)

Printed in the United States of America

For further information contact Made for Success Publishing
+14255266480 or email service@madeforsuccess.net

Contents

Disclaimer... ix

Introduction: Paradise Island xi

    The Satisfaction Zone xiv
    What is Your Definition of Success?................. xv
    Know the "Whys" in your Life xvi
    The Seven Seas.. xix
    Success and You.. xxi

CHAPTER ONE
SEA 1: Finances 1

    Timeless Financial Lessons............................. 6
    The Economic Levels of Society 10

CHAPTER TWO
SEA 2: Family 15

    The Sea of Family.. 15
    A Dark Place Called Fear 18
    Families Launch Us Across
    the Seven Seas of Life 21
    My Grandmother's Legacy 24
    Family Lessons and Overcoming Fear 26
    Timeless Lessons from Family 28

CHAPTER THREE

SEA 3: Increase Your Work Value.................... 31

    Professional Development.............................. 31
    High-Definition Performance 33
    Increasing Your Work Value............................ 38
    The Magic Fix Is in the Mix............................. 44

CHAPTER FOUR

SEA 4: Career 47

    The Relationship Circles 48
    Decision Making.. 50
    Organize, Systematize and Prioritize............... 52
    The Exit Plan.. 53
    The Blueprint for Success............................... 54
    Business Strategy... or Tragedy? 57
    Winning in the Game of Life............................ 60

CHAPTER FIVE

SEA 5: Social Networks 63

    The Ocean of Emotions 70
    Romance and Reality...................................... 70
    Rejection... 72
    Choosing Your Social Network Wisely 74

CHAPTER SIX

SEA 6: Navigating the Storms of Life.............. 77

    The Fear is Real... 79
    Stop Worrying and Start Living........................ 84
    Life in the Fast Lane 86
    A Tale of Two Possibilities............................... 90
    Dealing with Vultures...................................... 93
    Emerging from the Storms 95

CHAPTER SEVEN
SEA 7: Growing and Protecting Wealth 97

The Money Tree... 97
The Uses of Money... 99
Essentials of Wealth....................................... 101
Take Care of Debt.. 103
Managing and Tracking Your Wealth............... 106
The Formula for Winning............................... 108
Estate Planning Made Easy............................ 109
Protect Your Estate Plan 112
You're in Charge.. 114

CHAPTER EIGHT
You, Too, Can Design Your Life 117

Legacy by Design... 117
Fulfilling Your Passions.................................. 121
Creation 123
The Ultimate Plan.. 124
How to Enjoy Your Wealth.............................. 126
Sunset of the Journey 128
Vision, Precision, Strength 130

About the Author... 133
Appendix 135

Disclaimer

This book reflects my own personal experience. Financial results are not guaranteed and will vary with each individual and their personal situation.

Individuals must consider their specific situation including their financial goals, age, health, need for liquidity, current financial situation, risk tolerance, and their experience and knowledge of financial products and investments before pursuing any financial strategy. They should evaluate their financial strategy annually to take into account changes in their personal situation.

Individuals should consult with their own advisors for financial planning, tax and legal advice.

Financial strategies will vary with each individual, since strategies reflect an individual's current financial situation, age, future financial goals, need for liquidity, risk tolerance, etc.

An individual must qualify for life insurance and long-term care insurance via underwriting, and taxes are only one of the considerations when evaluating a financial plan.

Introduction: Paradise Island

When you hear the word "paradise," what first comes to your mind? Maybe it is an island getaway with a cool breeze and sunshine. Maybe it is a cabin in the woods with your significant other, with no one around for miles. Everyone's idea of paradise will be different, depending on their upbringing, cultural background, and social and economic status.

I want you to imagine you are given a blank canvas to draw and paint on and tell me: What would your picture of paradise look like? Who would you want to be with you in that paradise, and what would you create?

Now, I know that not everyone would draw their paradise to be an island, but for the purpose of this next section, we're going to imagine that it is. In pursuit of this Paradise Island in your imagination, we will be embarking on what I call the **working ship** that takes us across the Seven Seas of Life. The working ship has all kinds of people on it, doing different things for different teams. We call these careers. Some careers are very highly skilled and educated, where there are others that require fewer skills and knowledge.

However, each career has its role on the working ship, all necessary to take it from one harbor to another.

We work and serve others until the working ship stops at another harbor to pick up new workers and supplies. At each harbor, some workers depart and others come on board, following the natural ebb and flow of career paths. At some point, every ship will reach full capacity. The captain, CEO, and remaining officers must make decisions regarding which workers will stay and which will go. Decisions about hiring and firing are made in the best interests of the company — the entire ship of people. Those who are least productive and make less important contributions to the company will be let go. Others will leave due to changing career interests, illness, or retirement. Unfortunately, some people will need to come off the ship and be replaced by less costly workers. With this in mind, what if you must leave the ship before you are ready, and you are still far from your own Paradise Island? What do you do?

The reality of career setbacks is always a possibility, whether we want to recognize it or not. However, it's always possible to chart your course for Paradise Island at any point in your life. You will need to start planning now for how you will arrive and how you want to live on your own Paradise Island. You will never get there unless you take action, so don't sit around without purpose and become a victim of circumstances.

In the past, many workers all went to work for one ship — one company — after finishing school, and they worked there for many years. After they retired, they lived for a few years on a modest retirement in a paid-off home before they passed away. As of late, it is the norm to have several careers in our lifetimes — we work for multiple ships, and do not wait around to risk being replaced. We know that education must be ongoing in order to enhance our value as workers, and we have strong desires to experience more and do more. After our careers are well-established, our thoughts increasingly turn toward reaching Paradise Island. This is where we will enjoy our retirement years.

Many men and women in middle age no longer need to worry about just getting by or raising their children, so they begin to consider their life philosophy and what matters the most. They think about what they desire in life, and how they can enhance their Paradise Island, where they want to live the rest of their years. For example, they start thinking of a retirement place or a second home, or exotic travel destinations, or serving a cause or mission to help others. In their pursuit of what matters most to them, some will experience a midlife crisis and turn to new things and adventures. Some will turn to finding younger partners, some will buy Harley-Davidson motorcycles, some will have a getaway place, and others will turn to exploring the world.

Whatever your interest may be, you need a strategy and enough money to carry it out.

The Satisfaction Zone

While thinking about what your Paradise Island looks like, it's important to think about what gives you the most satisfaction and pleasure in life. We are all created differently, and we come to the world with our own set of gifts, talents, and personalities. Many say the greatest discovery is self-discovery, and if you are not working on your plan, you are part of someone else's plan. This journey begins by identifying what gives you satisfaction, finding things that provide great pleasure. Pay attention to your passions, and what inspires and excites you. Many retired people say "yes" to activities or causes that they do not truly enjoy. They have a hard time saying "no." The clearer you are on what you desire and what sparks your passion, the closer you will be to reaching satisfaction and happiness.

Life will likely be full of struggles and adversity for most people. Whether you are rich or poor, male or female, young or old, life is going to test you. While sailing the seas on the ship to Paradise Island, the winds will often blow in a direction you did not desire. When they do, it will be critical to harness the power of focus, paying attention to your passions and what you find most satisfying. Otherwise, you might get lost at sea. Don't let the songs of the Sirens lure you to crash into hidden rocks. Avoid being drafted to do work or take part in causes you don't really like or enjoy.

Make sure to figure out the main things in your life that give you deep satisfaction, and keep those clear.

For many years, my number one objective was to create multiple streams of income by age forty. When I accomplished that, I had a tremendous sense of confidence and accomplishment. I became known as a person who got things done. I was able to take charge of my life and become a leader; I was the captain of my ship. You, too, can take the helm.

What is Your Definition of Success?

Each of us has his or her own interpretation of what success means. Is success focused on our personal, professional, or financial lives, or is it founded on the accomplishment of a worthy goal? For example, my definition of **financial success** is to see a return on your personal savings and investments that allows you to support your lifestyle without having to rely on your wages. A body builder's definition of success in his own field is quite different — it is measured by physical capabilities and personal records in the gym. However, both require the pain of discipline, persistence, and the courage not to quit in the face of adversity.

The power of thought is truly remarkable. It can rally people together around a specific cause, and it can propel people to greater heights in their personal and professional lives. In order to nurture the power of thought, you need a different set of skills and good input. With good mental input, you can have good mental output. What do I mean by good input? For starters, reading books and listening to audio from leaders you aspire to be like one day. Charlie Tremendous Jones said it best when he said, "Most great achievers who evolved to greater stages in their lives think on paper and read books." Great leaders are readers. Your future will be changed by the people you meet and the books you read. In my lifetime, I have read quite a few books that have altered the direction of my life and helped me evolve into the person I am today.

Some books that stood out more than others and had a great impact on me are listed in the Appendix.

Know the "Whys" in your Life

Knowing the "Whys" in your life shapes your sense of purpose. Why are you at this point in your life, and what are you trying to accomplish? Can you list ten passions and desires you have, or is it hard for you to think about the future or dream? Answering the "Whys" about your life is essential to being successful. The concept of a purpose-driven life holds that you cannot succeed unless you have a purpose and goal. Purpose is when you have a clear objective; motivation comes from having that clarity and a strong desire to achieve it.

In order to journey across the Seven Seas to success, you must first connect your goals and desires to your **purpose**. For example, if your goal is to be financially independent and have streams of income that can provide you with the time and freedom to be with your loved ones and live in a place that you love, that provides **motivation**. Maybe you like the sense of achievement and want to have an impact on many people's lives. You may long to help those who cannot help themselves, using the money you have acquired. Those desires will also motivate you to success.

Clarity is half the battle here. Knowing our objectives and having a clear vision propels us to make our moves. These might be simple goals, but worthy ones nonetheless. One year, our family rented a cabin in Big Bear, California. One day, we were snowed in and couldn't even open the door to get out. I had just finished reading a book called *Think and Grow Rich* by Napoleon Hill. I was sitting next to the fireplace with a notebook, and my mind was racing with everything I had just learned through my time with the book. This book presents the premise that whatever your mind can conceive and believe, it can achieve. After completing the book, I came up with three simple goals. At the time, I had no idea that these three goals would become my focus for the next fourteen years. My three goals were:

1. Provide my family with the best lifestyle, comfortable home, reliable cars, trips, great food and entertainment, and excellent education and care.

2. Become financially independent so that I could have multiple streams of income, not just from my work, but from the return on my savings and investments. This would help me maintain my family's lifestyle. In other words, I would become financially independent and not rely on my wages for my livelihood.

3. Be successful at what I do and build a good career record in the financial planning industry. I wanted to grow in my company and advance, as well as building my income, with the goal of eventually earning six figures.

After I identified what I referred to as "The Big Three," I shared them with my family and a few friends and promptly went to work on them.

Now, it's your turn. Think about and write down three main goals for your life. They can be personal, professional, financial, health-related, or educational. We'll call these your "Big Three." These major goals will identify the direction you will follow and will make your life exciting, challenging, and incredibly rewarding.

As part of this exercise, ask yourself questions like: What do I love to do? What am I good at? What is essential in my life? Who do I love the most? What should I be doing, and why? My goals listed above were to provide a good lifestyle for my family, to make us financially secure, and to have a successful career. These are the essentials in my life. Answering these questions is critical when charting your course across the Seven Seas to Paradise Island. Once you have some goals, ask yourself whether these goals are big enough and if they are possible. If they don't seem possible, why not? If you think you can accomplish your "Big Three" alone, they may not be big or challenging enough. If you believe it, you can achieve it. Is your belief big enough?

Discovering your purpose is what I call "The Power of Why." During the design stage of your life's master plan, it is imperative to figure out the "Whys."

Why have I created these goals, and *why* do I want to achieve them?

Those are some of the most important questions in this book. People who have enough *why* — a purpose and a cause — can rally others and move mountains. The Power of Why will provide you with compelling reasons to keep going, creating a sense of urgency and clarity along the path. The "Whys" in your life are the energy you need to get to Paradise Island. Show me a person with enough reasons as to why he wants to accomplish something, and I will show you a success story in the making.

The Seven Seas

If you are a captain and I ask you to build a ship strong enough to navigate the Seven Seas of Life, how would you create the blueprint? What elements in the design will you highlight so the ship has the best chance of crossing the seas to create a good life and arrive at Paradise Island? The ship must be sturdy enough to withstand storms, flexible enough to make quick course changes when needed, large enough to comfortably hold all its passengers, equipped with the latest navigation devices, set up for efficient communication with ports and other ships, and capable of providing all necessities during the voyage. Life is a journey; a voyage. Your journey of exploring the Seven Seas of Life will not be without difficulty, but it is all worth it. You will not achieve great things in life without overcoming adversity and challenges. You will not want to get old and dwell on your misery or failures, but rather share the stories of your triumphs and successes.

Most journeys have an element of risk to them; your voyage across the seas will not always be smooth sailing. Life is an ocean of emotions and experiences; a sea of complexity that is full of hidden reefs, storms, and large waves. There are experiences beyond our ability to figure out, and sometimes you have to surrender to the thought that these are the mysteries of life. This place called Earth is a mysterious system; it's important to remember this while looking at majestic and awe-inspiring places you sail past on the voyage. We are truly shaped by the places and events we experience in our lives, but many will remain a mystery.

As you move forward on your journey, remind yourself that you are the captain of the ship. You have a say over your destination and what kind of sail you set. You must also be sure to know that the wind of change is inevitable. You will need a good compass, strong sail, and hard discipline in the Seas of Life. You must find strength and courage to face the risks and overcome the difficulties. Set your course toward a successful transit and keep the goal of Paradise Island clearly in mind. Arrive the victor in your life's journey, not the victim of its difficulties. Some people become unhappy as they grow old and blame circumstances or others for how things turned out in their lives. They sink into remorse over how their lives turned out differently than what they envisioned. You don't have to be among this sad crew. You can navigate your ship to happiness and satisfaction.

The Seven Seas of Life we will visit as we move through this book are Finances, Family, Increasing Work Value, Career, Social Networks, Navigating Storms, and Growing and Protecting Wealth. When you arrive at Paradise Island, you will realize the benefits of your course through the Seas of Life. Take out your notebook, computer, or phone and jot down your answers to the following questions:

What are your desired outcomes in each Sea of Life?

Take some time, make a list of each sea, and rate yourself from 1-10 with 10 being happy, content, no changes needed; 1 being not satisfied, lots of work needed ahead. Be honest in your answers.

The compass of your life is governed by your personal philosophy and values, and your quality of life will be directly correlated to the way you navigate these Seven Seas. With that said, maintaining a balance in each area of life will be critical. Just like a ship, if you are too heavy on one side, your chances of capsizing grow significantly.

Success and You

What is your definition of success? What is important to you about living an exceptional and satisfying life?

My definition of success is that you are loved and respected by your family, colleagues, and friends. You are guided by a strong personal moral code and a business philosophy with high integrity. You are well-organized and working toward the accomplishment of worthy ideals and a master plan — a plan that *you* have designed. You are committed to a lifetime of personal and professional achievement in your field. You are a person who leads from the front, gets things done, and walks the talk. I believe that success is by design, not by hope. Goals are dreams with deadlines and action plans, not just desires.

You, too, can design your life. A life lived by design is very rewarding. My purpose in writing this book is to help you design a career plan, a financial plan, a retirement plan, an estate plan, and a life plan. There are situations that come to us that are beyond our control and leave us hopeless, dejected, and sometimes furious. Mother Nature's fury, divine acts, crimes, and wars are things you just have to understand as being part of the mystery of life; we cannot figure out why they happen to us.

I acknowledge that many things and events can totally be out of your control. The key is to have a plan. You can make adjustments, change deadlines, replace the players in the game, and redefine priorities. There is safety that comes from creating multiple sources of income. Many years ago, I left a credit manager position that was paying a salary and entered into the world of commission jobs. At the time, I did not understand the value or the potential in creating multiple sources of revenue. I didn't understand how those sources can multiply over the years. One of the main factors that contributed to my wealth-building was being able to earn money from multiple and variable compensation plans that had many drivers of income.

We all have to start somewhere. After developing your major goals and objectives, you need to put a quantitative plan in place. Do not worry about where you are starting from, as long as you do not end up in the same place a year later. When I was 23 years old, I started a habit of writing out an annual net worth statement. Every year in December, I set my goals for the new year, taking a look at where I am currently and where I can grow. In the beginning, I had a $17,000 credit line and only $500 to my name. Over the years, my financial position substantially improved, and a bit later in the book I will share with you how I increased my holdings considerably and became debt-free (excluding mortgages). After spending many years working in the financial industry, I can tell you wholeheartedly that personal wealth is achieved when you pay attention to your numbers. I often feel perplexed when I see how people live their entire lives without dealing with their credit scores or budgeting. I think it is devastating.

There is often a clear gap between where we are and where we want to be. Looking at our world of possibilities requires clear vision, a master plan, clear and focused objectives, identifying what is missing, and determining what actions and strategies we need to master and adopt. Committing all these to your memory is a great idea in theory, but I have learned that if you do not put them down on paper, it's easy for them to stay in your memory as ideas and never get fleshed out. I cannot emphasize enough how important it is to keep notebooks and journals as part of the process. Great achievers think on paper (or any device that helps you keep track and keep a record). Before moving on, I encourage you to start a notebook or page on your computer or phone dedicated to this process.

You are a success story in the making. As captain of your ship, you are in charge of how that story unfolds. Creating your master plan and blueprint for success is the key to the ultimate achievement of your endeavors. Many years from now, the world will be a better or worse place because of your commitments and the impact you made. Many opportunities will reveal themselves to you; some you will understand in your earthly life, and some you won't. Regardless, the key is to create and become driven by your goals to make a difference in the lives you will touch on your journey.

To summarize, here are the tips to navigating the Seven Seas of Life and to arrive successfully at your "Paradise Island:"

- Define what success means to you.

- Write down your personal philosophy and values.

- Identify your strengths and build on them.

- Identify your goals and priorities in each Sea of Life.

- Put a quantitative plan in place with goals, priorities, and timelines.

- Set actions and strategies to accomplish these.

- Keep track of your actions and results.

Disclaimer: I advise consumers to seek legal and tax advice from their own legal and tax advisers. They should evaluate their financial strategy annually to take into account changes in their personal situation. Financial strategies will vary with each individual, since strategies reflect an individual's current financial situation, age, future financial goals, need for liquidity, risk tolerance, etc. An individual must qualify for life insurance and long-term care insurance via underwriting, and taxes are only one of the considerations when evaluating a financial plan.

CHAPTER ONE

SEA 1: Finances

C reating, accumulating, and protecting your wealth is what we will refer to as "Growing your Money Tree." As you do so, it is crucial to explore financial principles and develop a formula to help you achieve financial security and freedom, including how to manage debt and control your expenditures.

The first step is to work on a systematic saving plan until you have one year of income set aside in a liquid position. This is important if you should become unemployed. You should purchase a life insurance policy to replace your economic value to your loved ones and pay off any debt. This will put the protection they need in place in case something tragic happens. If you are overwhelmed at the thought of putting together a plan, the following five points are a good starting place:

1. **Create an emergency fund:** Most financial experts suggest that you keep six months' income in a ready cash account for unexpected bills or emergencies.

2. **Buy a life insurance policy:** This will replace your earning capacity in case you can no longer work, giving security to your loved ones.

3. **Make sure you have health coverage:** People can be ruined financially without a good health care policy, as this protects you in case of illness or injury.

4. **Get disability coverage in case you are ill:** A disability policy is an income replacement policy that covers a certain percentage of your annual income, and the money is given to you to pay your bills.

5. **Start a retirement account as early as possible:** The earlier you save for retirement, the easier it is because you will have more years ahead of you for the money to grow, and the magic of compound interest is on your side. The longer you take to start, the steeper the climb and the more money you have to put aside to reach the same results. Many people underestimate the amount of money they have to set aside to reach a good solid balance in their retirement account.

For example, I started saving for retirement when I was 25 years old, and over the years, we enjoyed a double-digit return or high single-digit return, ahead of inflation. We also used the dollar cost averaging method, a financial concept that allows people to put a fixed amount of money (installments) in the market, which allows us to purchase securities over a long period of time at good prices with a fixed monthly amount. It takes advantage of security prices being high and low and gives you a steadier outcome. My strategy relied on slow and steady wins over a long period of time. If your time frame is shorter, you may want to consult with a financial advisor for a different investment strategy.

Next, you'll need to answer the following question: What is your personal philosophy about losing money? Personally, I do not like to lose money. Have I? Yes, and every time I learned a lesson. Beware of the equities market, such as stocks, bonds, and options, including speculative ventures and commodities. The above strategy took me fourteen years to complete. I wanted to reach a point in my financial plan whereby the return on my savings and investments could support my personal and family lifestyle and pay for all my basic needs.

So, I'll turn the question on you: How is *your* plan working? Where are you in your financial sea? How are you doing?

A good test is to look at the last ten years of your earning life and figure out what your total earnings have been. Let me give you a scenario. Assume you have earned $200,000 a year for the past ten years — that's a total of $2 million. If you've only saved $100,000 of it, you're not going to be very happy! The question to ask yourself is, over the past ten years, how much of your money have you kept and how much have you spent, and are you happy with it?

If you continue to do what you've done in the past over the next ten years, you will get the same results (or worse). Are you happy with the results? If the answer is "no," what do you need to change, and when? If the answer is "yes," good for you.

How will you know if you are saving enough? I suggest you get a second opinion on the financial structure that you have set up so far and come up with concrete numbers to make sure you do not miss the mark. Do not make your plan contingent on other people. After all, it's *your* life.

Without designing a financial plan backed by a good strategy and working on it, you will most likely miss the opportunity to accumulate a fortune. The key is to work harder on designing your financial strategy than you work on your job, and you will set yourself up for big success.

Now, you should know from the get-go that a wealth strategy will undoubtedly challenge you. Some of your objectives will not be met for a long time, and some of your objectives will not be met at all. With this in mind, be sure to build a strong financial foundation. This foundation is based on being financially comfortable with resources enough to provide for your income needs. These resources could include adequate cash on hand, investments, retirement accounts, and insurance policies to cover future income needs. Make your financial strategy part of your life; much like your business plan, it is helpful to put it in writing and have checkpoints.

Unfortunately, the best strategies and financial foundations will never be enough if we do not tackle the enemy of consumer debt. If not managed correctly, it will become the sea monster that swallows your financial ship. It can even leave you with sleepless nights, high anxiety, and tremendous tension in your relationships.

Billions of dollars a year are made from high interest rates and fees charged by banks and financial companies. Once you accumulate over $10,000 in consumer debt, you become the victim of a gigantic web; caught up and tangled in it with no easy way out. These types of companies have teaser rates and promises of *90 days without interest,* luring you into their trap. Then, every time you purchase something, they try to sell you a card with hidden high interest rates that will cost you years of work and large sums to repay. If you don't pay off those balances, the finance charges begin, and the extra fees and high interest will apply. The small print on these card agreements has become smaller, and besides, when was the last time you read one?! The maximum allowable interest rate on a credit card is 29.99%, and the more you charge, the wider the web grows.

Here are some simple steps you can follow to avoid the credit trap:

1. Use the card when you need it, but pay it off as soon as you get the monthly bill. Don't let your interest pile up.

2. Spend money on items you have the money to pay for. I know it sounds simple, and it really is: If you don't have the money to buy it ... don't buy it.

3. Pay off the smallest bills first. Your goal is to reduce the number of outstanding cards before moving on to another step, and it will make you feel accomplished when you start to see those credit debts end.

4. Pay off the highest interest rate cards next.

5. As you're paying off your debt, don't stop saving. Pay yourself first rather than paying off your debt. I know sometimes it makes more sense to pay off the high interest first instead of saving; however, if you don't save, you're not setting yourself up for success in the future.

6. Resist the temptation to open up a card because of an enticing offer (and on an equally important yet unrelated note, always shred those offers to protect your identity).

7. Always refuse installment payments unless it's for your primary home; after all, the interest on your mortgage is one of the last deductions left that you can take!

By wisely managing credit card debt, you are improving your own lifestyle rather than contributing to the profit of these companies.

Timeless Financial Lessons

Finances are as important to living a healthy life as clean air and nutritious food. In order to navigate the Sea of Finances, you need a sound strategy and a good financial compass. From my many experiences, both positive and negative, I share the following strategy with you to help you avoid the same mistakes I made over the years. Luckily, the stakes were small, and the overall financial plan did not change much.

1. Pay yourself first; save first and spend second. Whether you contribute to savings weekly or monthly, just make sure you are putting away money as if you were writing yourself a check for your hard work. You deserve it!

2. Avoid lending money without security agreements. When you have money, other people will approach you for loans or to invest in their ventures. Be cautious about such generosity. If you decide to lend money, get notarized agreements with clear repayment plans. If possible, secure notes with a real estate deed, security guarantees, or valuables to back up the terms of these agreements.

3. Work hard on your wealth plan and growing your money. A wealth plan is your lifelong financial strategy to accumulate and grow your wealth. Though strategies may change with shifting economies, keep your long-term goals in sight and be disciplined in taking necessary actions to accomplish them.

4. Prevention is better than a cure, so limit your risk. Some of your strategies may end up losing money, such as investments that lose value. You may need expert help to assess the "down risk" or "up potential" of any investment. Remember, sometimes the return

of your money is more important than the return *on* your money.

5. Movement in the market does not mean achievement. Just because the stock market is up and the economy is doing well does not mean that your money is growing. Keep track of the value of your investments and holdings, taking results into account and making necessary adjustments.

6. Teach people how to fish; do not continue to fish for them. This adage also offers sound advice for handling finances. If you are advising someone on finances, you might just take actions for them instead of taking time to teach them how to do it. Having these conversations with other people will benefit them more than having things done for them. Don't let your pride or efficiency deprive others of important lessons.

7. Learn to say "no" without guilt; if it is too good to be true, generally, it is not true. Beware of the scammers. Take heed when something sounds too good to be true. Investigate, learn, and study the situation so you don't fall into a trap. It's far better to say "no" rather than lose your money.

8. When taking investment risks, know your stop-loss point, your down risk, and how far you can go. Some investments have high down risk potential; you need to know what your tolerance level is for possible losses. For example, would you be OK if you lost 30-50% of your principle? Make sure to establish the percentage

of loss you can live with, which is your stop-loss point. You should also calculate the up potential of investments that make the risk of loss worth it. As is often said, no pain (loss), no gain.

9. Diversification is the key; the more sources of future income you have, the brighter your future will be. The book by Robert Allen, *Multiple Streams of Income*, proposes that the more income streams you have, the richer you will become. Various income streams are earned wages and salary, rental income, dividend income, commissions, royalties, and many more. If one source dries up, the others keep going.

10. Stay out of consumer debt. The faster you get out of it, the better your future will be. Get out and stay out. Take the simple steps listed above to avoid the credit trap.

Disclosure: This book reflects my own personal experience. Financial results are not guaranteed and will vary with each individual and their personal situation. Individuals must consider their specific situation including their financial goals, age, health, need for liquidity, current financial situation, risk tolerance, and their experience and knowledge of financial products and investments before pursuing any financial strategy. Individuals should consult with their own advisors for financial planning, tax and legal advice.

The Economic Levels of Society

Financial concepts have far-reaching influences on society, especially in the United States, where class differentiations are less strong. European countries have a legacy of distinct classes, from the rulers and nobles, to merchants and artists, military professionals, and down to servants and peasants. These class distinctions have softened in modern times, but are still influential. Eastern countries often have legacies of caste structures, such as India, where Brahmins rarely mingled with statesmen, warriors, or artisans, while the lowest class of Untouchables were shunned by all above them. This structure has also been changing in recent years. In a democratic society with permeable status boundaries, the promise of advancement is always there. The United States uses wealth to a large degree to determine status, although many factors affect how a person is regarded, such as political leadership, entertainment idols, sports figures, religious icons, and intellectual or scientific accomplishments.

Using wealth as a measure of social status, people can be placed in various economic levels. There are several levels of economic lifestyles in our society, and you likely fall into one of these categories.

Level One: Survival

The primary concern here is to have the necessities of life like food, clothing, and shelter. Unfortunately, many people in this country of abundance are struggling simply to meet the most basic needs. Fear often dominates this level, combined with uncertainty and a high level of anxiety. Few can live happily when meeting basic survival needs is so tentative, although happiness is not impossible for some people at this level.

Level Two: Getting By

Being able to provide for basic needs with low wages, probably working two or more jobs, is the focus of people at this level. There is also a high level of uncertainty and generally high debt, with too little money left at the end of the month, if any. Most people with little education or marketable job skills are "just getting by." Entry-level workers, especially in food and service industries, fit here.

Level Three: Comfort

At this level, basic needs are provided, but there is no financial security. Generally, both partners are working, college-educated, and have good-paying jobs. They are relatively secure with a decent amount in savings. Home mortgages, dependents to support, and credit card debts are common. The family vacation is generally paid by credit card. Most of the time, people at this level are concerned about the future. They may have lost their position before, or they experienced unemployment periods and have used their savings to live on. Perhaps the majority of people in the U.S. are at this level, dependent on paychecks and unaware of or unprepared for their future financial needs. What will it take to continue this kind of lifestyle? Generally, people at this level are saddled with mortgages, car loans, and the risk of losing their jobs.

Level Four: Extreme Comfort

People who live at this level are usually highly skilled and college-educated, savvy about money, upper-middle-class, and often business owners. Thomas Stanley wrote a book called *The Millionaire Next Door: The Surprising Secrets of America's Wealthy*. In the book, he describes how many millionaires live simple lives while enjoying certain levels of luxury, taking vacations, owning financial products, having economic powers, and participating in charities. Such people are generally happier, more confident, and less worried about their jobs. They value the dollar and are wise about how they spend it. They have little fear about the future, and they are disciplined savers. They carry limited debt, mostly just mortgage debt, and pay their credit card charges and bills in full each month. Extreme comfort is the way to be. My wish is that reading this book will assist you in achieving this level.

Level Five: Luxury Living

These are wealthy people who live a luxurious lifestyle, with an abundance of money and large budgets, lavish spending with big houses and luxury cars. They're surrounded by a support team and a large network of professional service providers. Money is no object. These people are the "rich and famous," and they are rare. Society glamorizes these people. We see pictures of them and what they possess all over the place, both online and offline. Some are simply putting on the appearance of wealth, highly leveraged, and carrying a lot of debt. Very few of the truly wealthy worry about their economic future, and most of them are either self-made wealthy people or have inherited the money. Some of them are philanthropic in nature, while others are not. Luxury items generally surround their lifestyle. They travel first class, take six-star vacations, and are envied by society, family, and friends.

These characterizations of different economic levels of society are to give you a framework for thinking about your own financial position. Obviously, there are overlaps between categories, and not everyone at the lower levels is unhappy. Most people would agree, however, that having enough money to live comfortably and not worry about the future is a desirable thing. After reading about each level, you might be wondering, *Can I move from one level to another?* Of course you can. You are never stuck. You are not a Canadian goose, compelled by instinct and without choice that has to fly in the same direction at an allotted time.

When you are in a given level at one point in time, you don't have to remain there. You can choose to move to the next level. So, if you find yourself in Survival mode, like I did when I first started my earning years, you can move forward. I was working for hourly wages as a parking lot attendant and selling popcorn at the movie theater. But, I knew I didn't want to remain there, so I started a plan that involved saving part of my wages. Eventually, I accumulated enough money to attend school and acquire valuable skills for better jobs. I moved on to Getting By, and then to Comfort, and now I find myself in Extreme Comfort.

Let me reiterate: Just because you're at a certain economic level in society, doesn't mean you have to stay there. You have the choice to evolve to the next level. Why do some people evolve and others not? This has to do with our own mindset, covered in a future chapter. The important thing is for you to decide what economic level of society you want to live in and plan your strategies for getting there.

CHAPTER TWO

SEA 2: Family

The *New York Times* once printed a picture of six generations living in the same family; the oldest, the great-great-great grandmother, was 118 years old, and the youngest, the great-great-great grandchild, was three years old. It is very possible that we will each live a long life, spending as many as 40 to 50 years in retirement. But who is going to finance the future? This is a big question that warrants an entire book's worth of answers; however, the following is my attempt to give you the information you need to plan for your future.

The Sea of Family

Our families are the basis for experiencing the full range of what life has to offer. No matter how your family is made up, it is through them that you first experience love, learn acceptance, and are given a moral foundation. Families, whether just a few people, or large extended families of grandparents, parents, children, and grandchildren, provide the first step toward setting your life values. If you have children, taking your responsibility seriously as a mother or a father is critical. What governs a family is a bond of love and commitment.

The family is very important for many reasons, and you can think of it as the circle of life: When you are young and dependent on your parents, you receive care and guidance. Later in life, through old age or sickness, you may also enter another phase of dependency. The people you love often provide care then, as they are your first line of defense. For many elderly people, the family is their primary caregiver, generally a daughter, son, or sibling. Families often rise to that occasion, helping their elders have a better quality of life, surrounded by loved ones. To prevent family memories and history from fading in time, you can create an account for future generations using videos, pictures, journals, and trust documents. Trust documents, wills, and end-of-life instructions are especially important to create a legacy and pass it on to the people who mean the most to you. This leaves no doubts about your likes and dislikes and where you stand before and after you die.

Looking around our modern society, we see many broken families. The desire to maintain a strong family unit is slowly disappearing, and not only is divorce on the rise, but our elderly are left with no one to take care of them. This has a long, devastating effect on society and the social structure of our community. One of the fastest-growing industries is senior and adult care services, such as retirement communities, memory care facilities, assisted living, and adult daycare. Many seniors today are neglected, lonely, and broke — both financially and emotionally. Unfortunately, that statistic is not going to go away any time soon if we continue the way we have been living, as that is the price we pay for being an individualistic society.

People are now living longer, and if we desire to see a change in the Sea of Family, we need to work at it. Family is one of life's greatest gifts, and I believe there are ways we can start to rebuild after the shipwrecks so many families experience. How?

Well, for starters, it requires a time commitment and effort to reach out and nurture your family relationships. This must go beyond a text every few months or a Facebook comment on their birthday. Ask yourself: When was the last time you gathered your family together to celebrate a birthday, anniversary, or graduation? This might require significant sacrifices to hop on a plane or organize a family reunion. It might require you to front the bill for a family dinner. Whatever you have to do to bring your family together, I promise you; it will be worth it. Spend more time and money on the people you love and care about. If it is not you, then who? And if it is not now, then when? Family is where it all begins and ends, my friends.

A Dark Place Called Fear

One dark night, around 3:00 a.m., I woke up in a cold sweat, overwhelmed by fear. It was a nightmare that shook me — one with no ghosts, monsters, or natural disasters. It was merely a horrific dream wherein I relived every moment of my life, doing the same thing day after day. The same routine, same people, and same events repeated themselves without any changes, results, or different outcomes. After much contemplation, I realized this dream was likely the result of a movie I saw a few years before, in the 1990s. The movie is called *Groundhog Day*, and features actors Bill Murray and Andie MacDowell. It's a dark comedy about a weatherman and a beautiful young producer. The weatherman experiences the same day over and over again, living in a constant state of déjà vu.

The movie had a serious message, which caused me to have the nightmare. The message was about the fear of moving ahead in life and making changes. The cynical weatherman is stuck repeating that same day until he makes changes in himself to move from selfishness to becoming a benefactor of others. Many fears keep people stuck, such as fear of success, fear of loss, fear of rejection, or fear of failure. One of the deepest fears I had growing up was to be caught in a dark place that I could not leave. I was terrified of having to live a dark, dull life, never experiencing variety or the joys that life has to offer.

To move through and enjoy this journey of life, we need to control our fears. Life brings us trials and obstacles that I liken to the crashing of the waves in the ocean. The waves come with regularity; some small and some big. Many of us try to manage the waves, while some go to a dark place and try to hide from them. But what if we learned to embrace the waves, allowing them to crash over us and accepting them as a part of life?

Which begs the question: What is life really about? Is it about the lessons we must learn on our journey? Or is it about varied experiences we need to live through, and what we are to learn from those struggles and challenges? Are we spiritual beings having life experiences, or are we just super-developed mammals destined to play a part in the circle of life? Some people are simply trying to survive; others are trying to get to a destination or goal, while others seek job success and creating financial stability to live comfortably and provide well for their families. Other important goals in life are being loved, respected, and surrounded by family.

Our families give us the basic tools for handling fear and pursuing a satisfying life. When families are broken or alienated, these tools are often not provided. Then we may fall victim to fear that we cannot overcome.

Fear is a paralyzing agent. It can creep into our lives like a dark, evil spirit, and it will completely take over if we let it in. It can leave us feeling empty and scared, like being in a cemetery on a cold, dark night. Fear may push people to the brink, leading to such despair that they plot to take their own lives. Teenage suicide is on the rise in the United States, largely due to family disruptions that leave young people feeling isolated. A few years ago, we buried a young man who could have lived a beautiful life full of dreams and desires. It wasn't drugs or alcohol that pushed him to the edge; it was an emotional state that came from isolation. If someone close to him had reminded him of hope and encouraged him to pursue his dreams, it very well could have been a completely different story. However, without someone to invest in and guide them, teenagers can fall down the dark hole of hopelessness, wondering what their purpose is, what meaning life has, and lacking hopes and dreams.

What could happen if we came alongside these young men and women today, helping them create a vision for their life full of purpose and passion? They would have something to hold onto when the waves of life start crashing into them. One solution is to teach young people how to set goals and how to bring their ideas and work together.

If we can teach young people how to create vivid pictures in their imaginations of what their future can look like, they would be better able to overcome obstacles they will meet in their lives. This is one of the greatest gifts a family can give to their children. They could imagine what is possible in their future, hold vivid pictures of future goals, and develop strengths to stand up to fears of loss and failure. Instead of going underwater and sinking, they could swim through waves of life as they crash over them.

Just like these teenagers, you, too, have the right to pursue your dreams, desires, and happiness. We can all come out of this dark place called fear if we have the right tools. With a vibrant vision for the future, we can come out from underneath hopelessness and pain into a bright world of peace, prosperity, and happiness. Each of us has the power to create and the freedom to paint the picture of what we want our lives to be like, and we also hold the ability to control how vibrant it looks. In the age of technology, we are able to move past the vision boards of the past — made from poster board and magazine clippings — and use our imaginations with the internet to paint a brilliant image of what our life could be like.

Families Launch Us Across the Seven Seas of Life

Families instill moral and spiritual values in their children. These values are our rudder across the Seven Seas of Life. Many spiritual books talk about how God is within us, as is the power to create, all of which is a gift that was given to us when we were born. Our families help us develop our inner voice, or consciousness, which is powerful beyond what we can imagine. Our lives provide opportunities to figure out how to unleash the power of creativity that comes from this greatness within. It is this power that opens the doors to success and happiness.

Once vivid pictures are formed in one's mind and the objectives become clear, the motivation to carry out the plans are crucial. We should not only think of *what* we want to create, but also *how* to create it. As we sail toward our goals, we will be filled with joy, love, and hope in the process. There is a sense of personal empowerment in this. We are not just designed to love, but also to create, pursue, make progress, grow and expand; not to be stagnant. Having clarity and vision moves us away from the darkness of confusion toward new horizons of satisfaction. Think of the joy and excitement that explorers feel when they set out to discover new lands, the determination that keeps them going, and the massive sense of accomplishment when they arrive in uncharted territories. The journey itself becomes part of one's personal quest.

Our journey begins with conversations we have with our families, and moves to the most important conversation we could possibly have — the one we have with ourselves. Earl Nightingale once said that the strangest secret in the world is that you become what you think about the most. Our thoughts become our reality, and they manifest themselves in our lives. When we begin our planning, we need to do what I call a "brain drain" of our ideas, dreams, and goals on paper. Ideas organized on paper or a computer document become the foundation and future map that directs us to success. Before we begin to structure our plan, we should begin with our values and philosophy. For most, these are largely given by our families.

While sailing the Seas of Life, the four masts of your ship are the keys to a successful voyage: knowledge, skills, discipline, and finances. Without these, you cannot navigate your ship to your destination. Every successful voyage requires a good plan to chart the course and sound navigation skills. What is the foundation for setting the course of *your* voyage? What do you value most? Is it freedom to take vacations and be with your children? Is it having the finances to live a comfortable life? What is your purpose? Is it business success and financial security? What is the legacy you want to pass down to future generations? Is it work ethic and tenacity? Or is it the ability to dream big and see the impossible become possible? The clearer you are on this, the stronger the foundation for your life's journey, and the more beautiful and solid your inner vision will become.

Do not forget that matters of the heart are the fuel to our fire; the burning desire that urges us on to success. Here we go from the brain to the heart — the seat of emotions and strong feelings, love of those near and dear to us, and our passions. The heart is not always logical; you can give your heart to things that are not productive and might even be harmful. Once you have a passion for something, you will do whatever it takes to make it happen. These matters of the heart influence every decision we make, including who becomes part of our life and who does not. It's good to temper the heart with the wisdom of the mind's logic. Recognize when a passion is running away with you or leading you in the wrong direction, and use your brain to bring it under control.

There are three types of people in the world: those who make things happen, those who watch things happen, and the rest who wonder what the heck happened. Since you are reading this book, you are most likely one of the ones who want to make a difference and make things happen. You wish to win in life and make our world a better place.

But where do you start, and how? We need to begin with the end in mind. How would we want our lives to look as we near the end? Think of your life as a movie in which you are the star. What do you want to see in that film? What will be on your tombstone, and what are people going to say about you? How do you want to be remembered, and by whom? Are you planning to live a big life, a life full of variety; a life full of memorable experiences? Do you want to live to learn, to love and be loved, and later to leave behind a legacy for generations to come?

In my family, we call this legacy "between the dash." As you see, many tombstones have two sets of numbers — the year you were born, and the year you died. Often there is a line below for a short phrase, or something memorable about you. What do you want to be remembered for on this line "between the dash?" A life well-lived is a life that made a difference and had an impact on other people. Many people disappear in history, leaving little or no impact. Other people create monuments and buildings in their names, leaving a lasting legacy. What is your legacy going to be? It is up to you. Many years from now, most people will not remember you, but the world will be either a better or worse place because of your legacy. The difference you will make in the lives of future generations provides the basis for the short story, the memorable phrase about you that is carved on your tombstone.

My Grandmother's Legacy

My dad passed away at age 35, and my grandmother, called "Teta," moved my mother, brother, and me into her home shortly afterward. I was four years old, and my brother was only one. My grandmother was a true matriarch; a pillar of strength who loved me, raised me, and gave me the foundation to become who I am today. She ran a large household, managed the budget and all service providers, including multiple maids, and oversaw the shopping. She was in charge of family dynamics and relationships, setting the tone and upholding our values.

Teta taught me discipline, order, and organization. I learned how to keep a clean and well-organized home from her. She set high expectations, always seeking to bring out the best in me and everyone in the family. For example, my uncle, who was her oldest son, needed to touch base daily or every other day with her, or he would never hear the end of it. For me, this emphasized how important it is for families to stay in close contact with each other. On Sundays, everyone gathered after church for dinner in Teta's home. We all sat around the table, enjoying a wonderful Sunday dinner and sharing each other's company until she became very frail and could not host us all. This tradition of bringing all three generations together for regular dinners was then carried on by my oldest uncle, hosting us at his home.

Unfortunately, these traditions I was raised with were not fully carried on after the death of my mother and grandmother. We had moved from Syria to the United States, and I tried to hold on to the traditions for a while. But, due to distance and effects of Western culture, some of these Eastern traditions disappeared. The core family values, however, were continued.

Teta is the reason I am a loving father and grandfather and have never wavered in my love, support, and commitment to my family I provided for my family, including my wife and three children, whom we are both so proud of. They are college graduates, gainfully employed, and self-disciplined. They are people of high integrity, committed to their family, and supportive of their children. I spoil my children, especially my grandchildren, and love doing it.

Family Lessons and Overcoming Fear

What I learned from my family gave me the strength to overcome fear. No matter what your situation, the only way out of fear and a mundane life is to create a life worth living — a life where you can pursue your passion and realize your dreams. Fear will keep you stuck, holding onto things that do not move you forward. You won't make the changes you need to make, and this leads to a life of regret. Your journey to success will not be easy, and you will be challenged. You will encounter obstacles along the way, but they are lessons to learn from and ultimately bypass. You will have to adjust and make corrections along the way. The future belongs to those who prepare for it, and the future is where you will hopefully spend most of your time. It's up to you to do the work.

While finding my way in this world, I had to make course corrections, often learning by trial and error. One poor decision I made, based on emotions alone, cost me a great deal over the years. Now, I follow an organized process that brings logic and analysis into decision-making. Here are my steps for good decision-making:

1. Seek advice from people in the know. Listening to people without expertise and experience does not provide good guidance.

2. Determine what is under your control. There will often be circumstances or conditions that you cannot control, and some that you can. Get clear about which you can alter or change, and seek to understand the impact of those you cannot control.

3. Focus on your objectives, keeping them front and center. Do not allow yourself to get distracted by factors that do not contribute to attaining your objectives. You will only waste time and energy if you focus on peripheral things.

4. Bring thoughtfulness and creativity to your decision-making. By thinking outside the box, you may find that there are multiple solutions to achieving your objectives. This gives you options to consider and different routes to take, broadening your choices.

5. Organize your approach to decision-making. The questions to ask yourself are: What can I do, what can I read, and who do I ask for help? With these questions, you will be learning and gathering data, assessing your capabilities, and determining where to go for further assistance. It's always a good idea to write or record steps in your decision-making process; then, you can quickly recall and re-examine them, adjusting as needed.

Timeless Lessons from Family

We all learn timeless lessons from our family. Don't forget to thank your family for the foundation they gave you to create a successful future and a deeply satisfying life. Even if your family was not "perfect" and put you through lots of challenges, you learned valuable lessons and became stronger. Use your creativity to find gratitude, even for experiences of adversity.

My family provided many lessons that helped me lead a successful and satisfying life. In sharing some of these, I hope you may find that you learned similar things that were equally useful from your family. These are some of my timeless lessons from family:

Traditions. There is a reason why traditions persist in all cultures. Traditions bring families together and help us hold on to foundational beliefs. They preserve family continuity. Food traditions bring sentimental and physiological comfort to all of us. They maintain our links with our cultural backgrounds. Sharing traditional food and meals helps gather people around us and keeps us grounded. Cooking and eating together are forms of giving and receiving. Another tradition is sharing household chores and routines. This teaches children discipline and the importance of keeping things neat, clean, and organized. It creates a pleasant, inviting home environment, the opposite of what we see when families have hoarding problems. Food and other traditions have been core unifying forces in my family.

Loyalty. Being loyal to others is the basis of strong and lasting bonds among people. Relationships are formed that last a lifetime, and families learn to overcome differences and find the basis for continuing love. My grandfather used to take me to the spice market, where he would purchase spices for our home. Most vendors were located on one small street, all selling the same spices at similar prices. He always went to the same vendor, so I asked him one day why we were buying from that one and not the others. He told me that our family had purchased from this vendor for generations. My dad used to buy spices there, following the practice of my grandfather. That, he said, was loyalty in business. When you find businesses that have provided good services and products over generations, it is worthy of continuing the connection.

Shopping Wisdom. My grandmother had an approach to shopping that taught me about value. When I went with her to the farmer's market, we would walk the entire market and not buy anything on the way up the street. She examined the produce and checked on prices, but made no purchases. On the way back down the street, she would stop at a stall, point out what she wanted, and negotiate the price. So, I asked her one day why she did her shopping this way. She said that if you bought what you need from the first vendor and later found there was a better quality vendor with better prices, you would feel bad about your purchasing decisions. Wise shopping entailed looking over what was available and then deciding based on the best quality and price.

Paying the Right Price. I learned this valuable lesson from my aunt, who was wise in managing household repairs. Whenever there was a repair that would cost over $500, she always got three estimates from three different contractors. Then, she compared bids and qualifications to make the best choice. If the job was being done off-site, in a location some distance from her, my aunt would have pictures taken before and after the work so she could make sure that the contractor did a good job.

These were simple lessons from my family that helped me through my entire life.

CHAPTER THREE

SEA 3: Increase Your Work Value

Professional Development

Anyone who has moved up the success ladder will tell you that you need extensive study in your field. You can expect to spend thousands of hours obtaining an expert level of knowledge, then convert your knowledge into an action plan.

I'll never forget the moment one of my senior vice presidents (and bosses at the time) told me, "I am glad you have a college degree, that you have all your licenses, and that you are making a good living. But let me tell you this: Investing in professional and advanced designations in addition to continuous self-development will make you a fortune. I am going to require, as part of your annual evaluation, that you complete Chartered Financial Consultant studies and Chartered Life Underwriter designations. I want you to become a master in financial and estate planning."

In the beginning, I resented it. I did not want to use my personal and non-office hours to study such hard courses. Later, I resolved to do it. After 30 days of committing myself to studying — about the length of time it usually takes to develop a habit — I became accustomed to the routine and it was just another part of my life for the time being.

What I learned in those courses eventually helped me deal with some of our top financial advisers and assisted in building my personal work value, specifically in the area of tax planning. It opened the door to dealing with CPAs and estate planning attorneys by becoming proficient in their language. It paid big dividends in the long run, including gaining an expert reputation in my field of finance.

Whatever your field, continuing to study and expand your expertise is essential for advancement. Most fields are rapidly changing in today's world, and lifelong professional development is the way to keep up. I also encourage you to take further education in applicable financial literacy. No matter how you earn your living, you want to manage your financial assets in ways that bring you and your family a comfortable standard of living, as well as security in your retirement years.

High-Definition Performance

Being successful in business today requires what I like to call "high-definition" performance. Black and white television is long gone, and SD (standard definition) color TV sets have even started to slowly disappear. Can you picture yourself trying to get used to these old devices after watching movies in HD (high definition)? The same goes for business. Once you've experienced high-definition performance, it's nearly impossible to go back to the black and white of lesser levels.

So, what exactly is high-definition performance, and what does it entail? High-definition performance is doing your work at peak quality with sharpness, clarity, and precision. It requires an organized mind and a very specific formula to win in both the business and life game. Go back to your Big Three and remind yourself of the specific goals you have. Work out the finances by creating a budget, setting financial goals, tracking your progress, staying aware of debt and not letting it accumulate. Decide who is going to be on your professional financial team and why. Take ownership and responsibility and be realistic in your goals. Make a declaration and affirmation, and only share them with a few trusted people who love you and care about your success.

An example of a **declaration** is: "My master plan is manifesting itself daily in my life."

An example of an **affirmation** is: "I am loving the way I'm building toward my goals."

If you want to be an entrepreneur or highly successful in your profession, the value you bring to the marketplace determines your earning power. Remember, your earning ability is your greatest economic asset. You increase your value in the marketplace by charting and creating your master plan and working through it. This way, you will be able to predict your future to a certain degree. The reward is in direct proportion to what you bring in value to the marketplace — your work value.

Here are some questions to help take your business performance to a new, high-definition level:

1. What is my objective, and where do I want to be three to five years from now?

2. What is the reality of where I am now and where I want to go, and what strategy must I develop to get there?

3. How can I continually increase the value of my work?

4. Where do I need to invest my time to increase my cash flow? (Hint: It is in certain areas that you make most of your money.)

5. What kind of sacrifices do I need to make in the short term to achieve long-term success?

6. Do I have financial protection and a crash-proof net worth?

7. What am I doing to reduce my debt?

8. What should I be doing to improve my customers' experiences?

Society is constantly looking for new ways to do business, and businesses are looking for new customers who are interested in their goods and services. This is one of the big mysteries we are dealing with in the age of automation and technology. The system is on trial, and we do not know the future outcome of retail services when it comes to the online world, but we know this: We are creative, and we can adapt and evolve. The future belongs to those who prepare for it.

When I was a child, we had a black and white TV with a rabbit-ear antenna and three channels to watch. The picture was anything but clear, but we still loved it. I watched the *Mod Squad, The Love Boat, Bonanza, Roots* and *American Bandstand with Dick Clark*. These shows, along with great movies, gave me a feeling of enjoyment and pleasure. Imagine the moment I saw color TV for the first time and got to see all my favorite shows in color. I cannot even begin to describe how thrilled I was! The picture was not the best, and the definition was not what it is today, but it was a major upgrade from our black and white past.

Now, fast-forward to the age of HD. One day, as I was walking around a Circuit City store, I saw my first high-definition TV. I stood there with my mouth wide open for what felt like hours, mesmerized by the sights in front of my eyes. The vivid colors, the clarity, the speed, the beauty of the picture and how close it was to reality made me want it — in a bad way.

At that time, even VOOM TV only broadcast in high-definition for a few hours a day. It was owned by Mark Cuban, a genius businessman far ahead of his time. I later paid over $7000 to own that TV, and what a pleasure that gave my family and me! We had an extra five years of pleasure before it became a mainstream product. I could have waited, but why? It was more than just a TV; it was a complete paradigm shift. I couldn't go back to the "old way." The same could be said for our lives — once you start to live in high-definition, it is hard to revert back.

The time has come to make the change — to become a high-definition performer — for the same reasons: clarity, brightness, speed, and the overall picture quality of your life. As we've touched on already, clarity in where you're headed and how to get there can help you accomplish so much more in your life. It allows you to focus on what really matters: planting seeds in valuable and productive relationships.

Imagine you are the helmsman of a ship, steering it through a narrow passageway between cliffs. You see a flock of seagulls in the distance and get distracted. You turn from the wheel to watch the gulls, but in the process, you forget the original goal. This could cause the ship to go off course, or worst case, crash into the rocky cliffs. When you remember and are clear on your ultimate goal, it will help you not watch the gulls — rather, distractions that lead to unproductive or disastrous activities in your life.

Watching the seagulls is an exercise in futility. However, many of us do so, and even spend valuable periods of our life chasing after distractions. The gulls are the superfluous stuff; the things that will take us off course, and which we have little or no control over. If we refuse to acknowledge or identify such things, these distractions will take up time and effort better used to attain the goal. Keep your focus on the main goals of your life, and don't get lost in all the gulls (distractions) coming your way.

For example, many people discuss their desire for a promotion with their colleagues and other employees, instead of the bosses who can make it happen. We have conversations and gossip with the wrong people most of the time — people who have very little to do with the outcome — because we lack the courage to have it with the decision-makers or the people who can do something about it. Not only does this reduce our chances of actually getting a promotion, but it also costs businesses billions of dollars each year in nonproductive conversations. Ask yourself how every conversation fits with your priorities or goals, and whether it will help you achieve your objectives.

Many people I know think more about where they would like to be instead of assessing where they are. Just taking stock of where you are won't help without doing something about it. People who devote too much time to thinking rather than acting typically lack discipline and the hustle necessary to be successful. A friend once told me that success comes to those who hustle while they work toward the greater goals that will come in the future. We have to be OK with waiting for our actions to have results, but we can be working toward other objectives in the meantime.

So, how do you move your life to high-definition performance? I want to explore the steps necessary to move your life into a vivid, colorful place that is full of beauty. As I've been emphasizing thus far, you must have a clear purpose and reason why you are pursuing success. What is your intended goal? Get clear about it.

Now that you've made a list of goals that you want to achieve — the long-term first and the short-term second — in all areas, take the next step of putting them down on your calendar. Organize your goals in writing. Once you have them written down with timelines, you'll need to examine your current situation and assess what is missing to determine a course for moving forward. This will include creating a list of skills and knowledge that are necessary to reach your goal. Now you have a formal written plan with deadlines and a list of the people you need to seek out to get help in accomplishing your goals. Study your calendar and how you are going to incorporate all of these action items, when, and with whom. Following the above guidelines will help you advance your journey into a new and higher level of performance.

Increasing Your Work Value

Here are some questions you need to ask yourself about increasing your value in your professional work. Take your time to answer these questions on a separate page. Be true to yourself and be honest.

1. How can I continually increase the value of my work?

2. How can I best invest my time to increase my income?

3. What can I sacrifice in the short term for long-term success?

4. What amount must I set aside for long-term financial goals?

5. How can I reduce my debt and live a debt-free life?

6. What am I doing to increase my income-earning ability?

After answering these questions, you may realize very quickly that you have much more work ahead of you. But, the good news is that the best time to do the work is *now*. The longer you wait, the harder and steeper the climb. Here is a tip from my mentor Jim Rohn: "Work harder on yourself than you work on your job."

The plan above will be your blueprint to financial success from this point on. Keep looking ahead; not to the people on your right and left. Don't get distracted by someone else's plan. It is always better to work on your own course than to be part of someone else's.

We're going to now turn our attention to using professional development to increase your work value. You will be embarking on a self-examination journey that will evaluate your skillset. What, if anything, are you an expert in? The higher you want to go in life, the more you need expertise or specialization. So, why become an expert? People like to call on an expert should the need arise, and they are willing to pay a premium. Over the years, when I became responsible for managing matters I was not familiar with, I had to pay premium dollars for experts on those subjects.

I read once that to be an expert in a field, you should expect to spend at least a thousand hours on a subject. So, when was the last time you spent a thousand hours studying a topic or a subject? We spend thousands of hours on the superfluous stuff, but with concentrated effort, we can choose a relevant topic and get to work on increasing professional value.

Today's marketplace requires experts. You must invest time and effort and energy into studying and taking professional courses, personal development courses, and skill-building classes such as communication and business management.

Once I made the decision to study and pass courses in financial and estate planning, I watched my confidence go up and my income skyrocket higher than ever. This wasn't simply because of the courses, but because of what I became in the process: more knowledgeable and able to implement that knowledge in real life. Don't shy away from attending conferences, classes, courses, and joining professional organizations as you endeavor to become an expert. You will not only be able to make additional connections, but you will accumulate real-life knowledge you likely won't be able to find elsewhere.

When I obtained my Chartered Financial Consultant and Chartered Life Consultant designations from The American College of Financial Services, it gave me a tremendous sense of accomplishment. I had the same rush when I passed every qualifying exam for the seven professional licenses I hold. Having licenses and a professional designation in a particular field makes you more confident and will make you more money. Many individuals I know start these courses but never finish; they shy away from the difficulties and the time necessary to complete them. They would rather chase the gulls of distraction. Make good on your promises to yourself and others; it is your badge of honor.

Across the board, employees today have higher-level degrees than they did in the past. Having these degrees, licenses, and professional designations are the best way to guarantee your continued work value. In the last few decades, we have seen layoffs and replacement of functional employees' positions with technology, with many jobs outsourced to developing countries. More of this can be expected in the future, with the spread of artificial intelligence and robotics. The average employee today switches jobs and careers between seven and eleven times during his or her lifetime. The days where someone can work for the same employer all their life and have a pension and retire comfortably are almost gone. Now we see too many employees displaced before they can retire. They will be facing too much time left in their working life when the money runs out.

Every person has what I call a *work shelf life*, which is becoming shorter and shorter for many, leaving them vulnerable to economic and financial setbacks. They may face extended unemployment periods with a high possibility of becoming dependent on the welfare system. Many people are just one paycheck away from welfare or homelessness.

Everyone has only so many years after finishing their education to earn money. Their work shelf life is the time when they make a living, are productive workers, and create value to the marketplace. Getting additional degrees and specialization extends your work shelf life. During your best earning years is prime time to set up your financial future, so when paychecks stop, your income does not.

One way to extend your work shelf life is to become self-employed. For most people, being self-employed is a high-risk prospect. To a certain degree, they are seeking the security of a weekly or monthly paycheck, and they do not want to take on the variable income and compensation that comes with self-employment. That being said, I have a very different perspective: the more sources of income, the higher the security factor. You have a greater ability to have multiple income sources when you are self-employed.

So, let us examine this: most of the time, an employee has one or two sources of income, such as a salary and a bonus. But a self-employed professional with highly specialized skills often has multiple streams of income and many customers. An employer can take your job away from you.

If you work for yourself, a few customers can fire you, but there is little chance that you will lose all your customers all at once. Your degrees, skills, expertise, specialization, designations, and licenses are better security than a single job. Those things stay with you regardless of where you go. As long as you are able to bring value to the marketplace, that is the key to secure employment. Your future economic security will come from the value you bring to customers and clients.

An attitude of entitlement will do little to increase your work value and work shelf life. Often people have a sense of entitlement, feeling that other people or society owe them sources of support without earning that right. This attitude does not lead to success. For those wanting to achieve high-definition performance, it's important to remember that the work value and services you bring to others are keys to success. No one can do it for you.

Regardless of whether you are self-employed or are a long-standing employee of a big corporation, you cannot get around the fact that you need to work hard to keep moving forward. I've heard some employees and representatives who are not attaining their goals say, "I am doing my best. I cannot help it, but ..." Sometimes doing "your best" is not enough when you are not seeing the results you want. Results, or the outcomes of your actions, are the final judge. Intentions are not enough; you must develop the necessary skills, expertise, and discipline. So, what do you do if you find yourself stuck, and how do you fix it?

The Magic Fix Is in the Mix

Fortunately, there are several solutions or fixes you can turn to when you get stuck. Asking yourself some important questions will help clarify your direction and where to turn.

1. What can I do? Based on your knowledge and skill-set, identify actions you can take to get unstuck.

2. What can I research? Do your own research first before asking others for help. Today, access to information is easy and fast. You might discover just the right solution at your fingertips.

3. What does it cost in time and money to fix? Fixing problems requires time, money, or both. Evaluate the cost before making a commitment to pursuing the fix.

4. Who do I ask for help? Asking someone to help with the fix is the last thing you should do. Many people you might turn to don't have the expertise. Going to several people with the same question can be a waste of time. Don't seek answers from those lacking expertise or power to make changes.

Sometimes, you may have to do all of the above to find the solution — the magic fix is in the mix. The world is full of ideas, and an idea not acted on is not an action plan. The work begins when the action plan is implemented, and the fix is attained when it is completed.

While you are navigating the Sea of Increasing Your Work Value, pursuing professional development, and trying to find solutions to extend your work shelf life, every once in awhile, you will face a massive crashing wave. This can be a major work problem, or a life crisis. Try to follow the steps outlined here and figure out the best outcome. Stay focused on your objective and don't get off course; try to set sail through the rough seas and keep the ship's bow cutting through everything that is thrown at you. If the problem is too big to solve by yourself, you will need to seek help. Once you've done research and consulted with experts, your fix may become clear. If the problem reaches an impasse, the first step is to negotiate for a win-win solution. If negotiation fails, then seek arbitration or mediation. The last alternative should be to litigate. In the most complex of cases, you may need legal assistance and resort to the courts to reach your objective. Focus on the objective, and do not lose track of it. Set aside your ego and focus on the desired outcome, but do not delay or ignore the matter; keep your eyes on the prize, the final objective.

When the fix involves asking someone for help, remember that maintaining good relationships is important in the long term. Our life is a series of conversations; some with ourselves, some with others. Value the power of these conversations and have them serve a higher purpose — to bring you closer to your goals and objectives. Talk about what is important and seek to truly understand people, because they also have an agenda and objectives. By helping enough of them, you facilitate a path for them to help you.

The final objective is to increase your work value consistently as you sail the Seas of Life. Remember that your work shelf life will not last indefinitely. Make the most of your earning ability while there is opportunity. Keep financial goals in mind, and plan wisely for a secure financial future for yourself and your family. Navigating through the storms of life — the setbacks and crises that everyone faces — is further addressed in a later chapter.

CHAPTER FOUR

SEA 4: Career

In my experience as a business service provider, I've learned to keep in mind that success in business is *not* all about you. It is bigger than you, and the business is all about the clients, getting to know them, and showing them that you're the most reliable person to be entrusted with their professional dealings. At times, people will do things for others out of a sense of belief in them or a sense of obligation, and it usually shows when you're acting without passion or real interest. Mutually beneficial relationships are critical to your business success.

You will never have a second chance to make a first impression, so you must be sure you make a good one the first time around. A few years ago, I was referred to an attorney in my town by one of the reps who worked for me. The attorney arrived late to our first meeting, dressed casually in jeans. Spoiler alert: I never met with him again. If he treated our first meeting so casually, I reasoned that he would likely treat my business the same way.

What can we learn from that meeting? Your reputation — the cornerstone of your career — is on the line from the first time you meet with someone. Show up dressed to impress, be confident in the value you offer, and treat every opportunity as if it were your livelihood on the line. This is how my CPA kept my business over the years. He is attentive, returns my calls promptly, always shows up on time, and is readily available when I need to meet with him. I gladly pay his fees with no questions. Over the years, I have hired and fired many professional service providers for not living up to these expectations. Your reputation and image are critical to your future success, so give it your best shot no matter how small or large the opportunity might be.

The Relationship Circles

These are the circles of people that you surround yourself with: the inner circle, the second circle, and the outer circle.

Your **inner circle** (A list) would be the people you deeply trust and can rely on. If their name popped up on your phone in the middle of the night, you would pick it up. You know that you can count on them, and they can count on you.

Your **second circle** (B list) consists of the people you are close to, but wouldn't necessarily call if there were an emergency (and vice versa). These are the types of people you most often have professional relationships with, but likely have a backup plan when it comes to them pulling their end of a bargain.

Your **outer circle** (C list) would be those you consider acquaintances or basic business connections. These are the people you don't usually pick up the phone for or keep close tabs on. However, a lot of people in the outer circles do business with each other.

A helpful tool in thinking about these circles is to keep a list of those who are most trusted and reliable. If someone is not on your A list, move them to an outer circle. I keep track of my circles in a journal I update quarterly, or the very least, yearly. You could either do the same or list them in an online database. Anyone who is successful in business needs a professional team of advisors and trusted experts, which are your A and B lists. If you want to do business with the C list, there are a few things to keep in mind. These are people you should evaluate carefully and choose to work with on a limited basis before you consider them trusted enough to be on the inside. If your finances and business workings end up in the wrong hands, the results can be incredibly frustrating, costly, and stressful, to say the least. Beware of people who might use you for their own ends, or who might be inept businessmen, because there could be long-term consequences.

Most importantly, you must limit your losses and cap their fees at a certain point when things start to go wrong. Every contract is negotiable. Make sure that you clarify the objectives and anticipate the possible risks right at the beginning of the relationship. Putting the wrong people in the wrong place in your life can destroy you financially if you are not careful. Do not be afraid to fire someone who is not serving you in a way that benefits you first and themselves second.

When it comes to managing your finances and properties, it is important to take legal advice from the appropriate lawyers. It's always possible that a conflict or complaint might arise. A good principle to follow is mediate first, negotiate second, and then mediate again. If you must, litigate last. Many attorneys make their living from long and complicated litigations, but your business can suffer as a result of a bad and greedy attorney.

Decision Making

You are the CEO of your business, professional, or personal services. Take ownership, hold yourself accountable for your actions and decisions, communicate expectations, inspect results, and hold your people accountable for their actions. You are the leader! When the job is well done, your people will say "we did it" and feel proud of their accomplishments. Give credit to those who work for you and recognize and reward excellence. Don't take credit for other people's work. In the end, it is not the results alone that count, but what you will become as you proceed on that journey.

There is discipline in the art of negotiation and in dealing with people, especially those who are difficult to work with. You must have the courage to take on the challenging conversations and stay on topic to reach the objective and desired outcome you have in mind. In difficult situations, let your moral compass and foundational values be the guiding force in making the tough decisions and moving forward. What is the desired outcome? Let that be your rudder.

In business negotiations, many people lose track of this point — reaching the desired outcome — and end up in what I call a rat hole, which leads to nowhere and distracts from the main topic. Achieving the desired outcome should be the objective, but getting to understand the other person's point of view is a close second. You need to use your social intelligence in this task. Keep in mind human limitations and shortcomings. Agree on the terms in writing; the human memory is not enough to recall every detail for the long term.

Another crucial thing for CEOs and business owners to keep in mind is, "Cash flow is king, not just cash." You must find a way to make sure cash flows in, every season and every week. You are the business owner, CEO, entrepreneur, salesperson; you are the rainmaker. Your decisions are responsible for bringing the money to the business. You may falter at times, but what does that matter? How soon you bounce back is predicated on your willpower and the reasons why you are doing what you're doing.

Organize, Systematize and Prioritize

When setting yourself up for success, two of the most critical components are organization and prioritization. I've found that having both a master project list and weekly project list (and understanding how to track them both) is incredibly helpful. Over the past 35 years, I have developed a weekly tracking sheet for my "to do" items: a calling list and a follow-up list. A checkmark next to an item means it is done, and a circle means I want to carry it over to the next day or week. I also developed an annual plan and a quarterly plan, listing and identifying priorities alphabetically.

Over the years, I learned to tackle the most difficult items first, which I think played a major role in my success. I learned to delegate and hold people accountable by creating and storing the delegated assignments in an electronic file as well. Create a list of tasks that need to get done, set priorities and timelines, and assign them to yourself, your assistants, and other staff. You will quickly realize that other people's sense of urgency and timelines are likely much different from yours. For this reason, it is critical to give them deadlines and hold them accountable.

The mark of an effective leader is the ability to get things done. The marketplace will reward you for having made good decisions and for being bold. Expect good performance; some employees will rise to the occasion while others will not. If people are floundering and you've given them the opportunity to improve, but they continue to miss deadlines and fail at task fulfillment, have the courage to let them go. Remove yourself from ineffective relationships and move on.

The Exit Plan

I recently watched a movie where the hero, an undercover police detective, entered a European café. Before he selected a table, he checked the place out thoroughly. He looked around the room, located the back door, made sure he sat with his back against a wall, and chose a seat near the exit in case of an emergency or an anticipated unfriendly action.

Unsurprisingly, that is exactly what happened — he was attacked. Most of us never think about an escape plan, or what I'll refer to here as an "exit plan." Most business owners do not; they simply plan for and spend all their resources on getting their business underway. However, it is equally as important when entering into a business to make ready an exit plan, just in case. Losing a big client, facing new regulations, losing key people, lacking the necessary cash flow, or facing an unexpected lawsuit can all contribute to quickly losing a business.

Not all exit plans are for going out of business. Successful businesses also need such plans for when the CEO or owners no longer want to carry on the work. They may want to retire, or to move into another field or venture.

Planning how to transition a successful business to its next owners is also important.

The key to developing an exit plan lies in the middle of working on your primary business plan. Preparing for an exit plan does not necessarily mean something wrong is guaranteed to happen, but being ready for possible setbacks is the essence of a sound plan and provides a sense of security. Thinking about where the business might be going in the future is being farsighted. Making exit plans is good business sense. Every prudent business has a contingency plan, so don't think having one will jinx your business. Precaution never stops us from doing anything successfully, just like having your seatbelt on in a moving vehicle does not mean you will have an accident. Craft that exit plan and add it to your primary business plan.

The Blueprint for Success

When it comes to financial success, intellectual capital is the name of the game. This includes your education and specialty skills, as well as your abilities to analyze and anticipate directions in your business or professional field. Your will to succeed, determination to meet goals, discipline, and ability to handle setbacks are also an important part. How much intellectual capital you have and how you put it to good use determines how far you can go. The choice is yours. You can be a hunter looking for the next meal every day (Survival Level), or you can build your traps and a system that can work for you with the right knowledge, education, skills, skills. It is a critical ability you need to have to compete in the Information Age.

Your attitude in approaching business success is important. Focus first on the customers' needs, rather than your personal preferences. By providing high-quality services to others, finding an unfulfilled need, and helping enough people meet their needs, you can get what you want in business.

The first element of business success is clarity and focus. Focus on your objectives and what you want to accomplish in terms of knowledge, skills, and efforts. As I described earlier, specialized knowledge is tremendously helpful. The second element of business success is to have a written business plan and strategy. Remember, without a clear road map, it will be impossible to get to your intended destination. However, how to get there from here requires strategy, creating productive action plans, as well as an urgency to accomplish the set plans. Put all of these elements together, and you get what I call the blueprint for success. This blueprint is your business plan that also includes identifying people who can help you achieve success. Their role is as important or more important than yours.

To kick start your journey to business success, here are the seven steps to creating your blueprint for an effective business plan:

1. **Where You're Headed:** Put down clear objectives in writing, along with specific reasons behind each objective. Prioritize these objectives.

2. **How to Get There:** Write down specific goals, such as landing 20 new customers in the next year. Make sure you are attaching a deadline to each so you can track your progress.

3. **Game Plan:** You'll need written strategies for how to achieve specific goals, and working documents that are a punch or to-do list according to priorities. Add other project details here.

4. **Co-laborers:** Write down the names of people who can help you implement your goals and business plan, remembering the Relationship Circles.

5. **Timeline:** Think about specific events such as trade shows, events, or conferences you want to attend and write down some weekly action steps for each.

6. **Resources:** Make a list of helpful resources, data, and references that will help you get to your intended success. This might include people, places, and websites for the information you need.

7. **Summary:** This will be your project summary and outcomes in expected steps, with each step being a measurable action in your timeline.

Creating a blueprint for success is an art. There are business people that I call the reactive kinds, who constantly wait for someone to tell them what to do. That is not you. "If it is meant to be, it is up to me" is the philosophy of a successful business person.

Business Strategy ... or Tragedy?

We live in a quickly changing world with access to information on an unprecedented level, unlike any other time in history. Doing business under these circumstances is difficult, and it is only getting harder. Gaining access to people outside the internet and phones has also become difficult as we have barricaded ourselves behind our smart devices and computers. Consumers have purchased other services and devices to shield themselves, such as caller ID and spam detectors. There is a "Do Not Call" list and spam filters, and we rely heavily on online purchasing. It's almost possible to go about our days without any human involvement or interaction. Many jobs are being replaced by programs and artificial intelligence. So, what about the human element and engaging the senses in a conversation in order to achieve consensus and do business?

It is the human element and how you interact with people that will either lead to a successful business strategy or result in tragedy for both you and your customers. Our increasingly depersonalized world and widespread internet communications make it difficult for us to truly *see* other people. Many businesses and marketing organizations are spending billions trying to reach potential customers, much of it on social media and internet communications. While all this is necessary in our electronic era, it will never replace direct relationships with other people. Keep in mind that business depends on sales; we could say that in a business, nothing happens until someone sells something. Of course, there are many steps to making the sale, but selling something is the desired result or outcome.

So, how do we find customers, people interested in what we have to offer? We know that people have dreams and needs, and we must find a way to reach these people and help them. We know the human mind can create solutions, and that is where we are going to find the answers. Solutions within our reach must meet the needs of customers. I believe that advocacy is one of the solutions, along with strategic alliances among service providers. But, what do I mean by advocacy? Advocacy is seeing and understanding customer dreams and needs and offering ways they can realize them. In order to advocate well, you must ask key questions to find out where people stand. When customers are clear about these, then you can speak effectively on their behalf.

For example, employers cannot advocate well for their employees about benefits needed. Employees don't say to employers, "I need health benefits, a 401K retirement plan, and paid sick leave or maternity leave." As a financial planner, however, I could advocate those benefits for workers to their employer. I could explain why these are beneficial to the company. In very large companies, unions may serve as advocates for these benefits.

Take another example of advocacy. In a family, the children will not line up and say to their parents, "Make sure to plan so I can have a college education! Make sure you have an emergency fund so we will be taken care of if you can't work." The non-working wife might not be able to say, "Make sure you have a plan for income if something happens to you. Put aside money for us to live well in retirement." But I can come in and advocate for them as the family's financial planner.

However, in order to advocate for people effectively, you have to be very clear about your values and foundation, and you will want to advocate for people who are also clear about these. The key to successful business strategy is that the customers, be they a business or a family, cannot speak effectively on behalf of those depending upon them. They need an outside viewpoint, an expert with the required knowledge and skills, to best fulfill their dreams and needs.

For you to be able to advocate well, you must ask key questions to find out where your customers and those depending on them stand. Find out what is important to them about life, family, money, career, and success. You can only do so by meeting face to face and having conversations. You must be clear about what you stand for and what you have to offer and help them be clear on what they want. You'll need a dynamic introduction as to who you are and what you offer, and utilize all methods available, including video, email, third-party testimony, and attractive and easy use of websites with plenty of facts about you. Establish an early agreement before you do the work. That way, when you find solutions, you will have the basis for doing business; otherwise, you may find yourself doing the work as they buy directly online from someone else. Remember that the most essential task here is to create and retain customers, so your business strategy is a success and not a tragedy.

Winning in the Game of Life

Creating a successful career is only one aspect of life. The key to winning in the game of life is to have balance by taking time for yourself, time for others, and time for your career. The game of life is not simply about scoring the big career win — rather, it is a multifaceted victory. Just because you won a record once does not mean you won in all of life. The game of life is about career consistency and building long-lasting loving relationships. Some people may win a record accomplishment at work but lose their family and leave behind broken relationships. Others become so focused on the other people in their lives that they lose their careers. Another group may be so self-centered and selfish that they end up alone and miserable. Building your team of people, friends, and loyal business partners is the key. The power of your influence and presence will spread and help you achieve what you really want. The next step in your process is to recruit talented people to be on your team. If you think you can do it alone, your goal is not big enough. You will reach a level of complexity and stagnation that will halt your growth. There is nothing wrong with surrounding yourself with smart people with strong personalities; in fact, it is an advantage.

Here are some helpful tips for building a strong team:

1. Begin with highly talented people who you like. The talent and expertise of the team members is more important than what they do.

2. Look for people who share and value your vision. It is essential for the people on your team to support the vision you have and the master plan you develop.

3. Look for people who can develop good habits and consistency. Good work habits and discipline are required to have a winning team. One-hit wonders and inconsistent work are detrimental to your team's efforts.

4. Philosophical congruence is a major factor. Business philosophy is the guiding system of any successful team. People with different work philosophies can create dissent, and they may later go in opposite directions. It's highly advised that you check out the philosophical compass of team members in private conversations. This will help avoid dissent and ensure congruency.

The collective result of many work conversations determines the outcome of team functions and moves it toward winning the game of life. Teamwork requires commitments, and bosses must ask for this clearly. Asking for commitments and having strong and open conversation requires bravery and honesty by both parties, and healthy confrontations are required in high-value relationships. If you are on the receiving end of a hard conversation, be silent and listen intently. Healthy and transparent conversations are necessary for building any work team so they can work together for a common goal.

For many years I managed all kinds of personalities. Be careful when selecting people on your team who are too focused on themselves or too focused on others. They are equally problematic in terms of being productive members of your team. You want a person who can balance time for themselves, time for others, and time for their work. In the same breath, be aware of the phonies in life; they give praise without sincerity, flattery without substance, and comments without feelings. They are the distractions you do not want to invite into your team. They are not assets in winning the game of life.

In this section, we visited what it takes to build a successful work team. We examined how to resolve problems and what it takes to win the game of life. Earlier, we discussed the importance of relationships, decision-making, handling big issues, and having good business strategies. With these tools, you can have superior business performance and outstanding results, leading to success in the Sea of Career.

CHAPTER FIVE

SEA 5: Social Networks

We are all born with an intrinsic need for human connection; to have healthy and long-lasting social relationships. For our ancestors, having a closely connected tribal network was necessary for survival. Caring for each other through various forms of love is the glue holding social networks together.

We spend a good deal of time and effort seeking, holding onto, and hoping for more love. We want to hold onto our existing loving relationships, and to seek new ones over time. In contemporary society, our social connections have become difficult to maintain, in good part because we live much of our lives online. What happened to the tribe, since we are social creatures by nature? We have moved from a collective society to an individualistic society where many people don't fit in; they are socially awkward and find it hard to sustain relationships. Because humans are social animals, and our brains are wired for social networks, those who are isolated and estranged often take out their anger against society through violence or smother it through drug addiction. We have only just begun to see the side effects of an overly individualistic society.

Some people will take advantage of our deep need to connect. Leaders of charismatic religious groups or cults are in powerful positions to exploit lonely and disconnected people who feel weak and fearful on their own. Disguised as spiritual love, they offer a form of "quid pro quo" to socially hungry people by taking them into the group, essentially saying you can belong if you follow our ideology and beliefs, and give up your own thinking. They also drain money from their followers, supposedly in service of the ideology, which can be dangerous. In actuality, the leaders mostly line their own pockets.

The need for people to connect is not going away; it is now greater than ever. We have seen many forms of social networks — some culturally based and others based on communities, shared group interests, and professional focus. As with all human groups, there is a need to visit, connect, and support each other. That is one reason why many small retirement communities are popping up everywhere.

The retirement community phenomenon has touched most families. In my family, we watched one of my relatives become disconnected over a period of time as he reached his late 70s. His body was frail and he was losing weight, becoming isolated and speaking less and less. When he moved with his wife to a combination retirement facility / assisted living community, we thought things would certainly get worse. To my surprise, a few months later, when my wife and I visited, he looked healthier and happier than I had seen him in years! He had even gained over ten pounds. We asked his wife and his daughter what had happened; it turns out that his change in mood and behavior was all about social connections. Once he was around people more, engaging in day-to-day activities, his overall health and mood drastically improved.

Looking back over the years, we see that most societies were thriving when there was a sense of community. Today, some of the social and civic groups that help create community do not even meet in person, but rather over the internet. They maintain chat room connections, sometimes operating under hidden identities and fake profiles. The social and technological barriers we have built are preventing us from having the very experiences that make us human beings. We have gotten to the point where neighbors do not know each other or say hello, families and relatives rarely see or talk to each other, and children living away from home feel it is an inconvenience to talk to their parents. When we email or text or IM our family and friends, we cannot see, feel, and smell the connection. We lose the sensory experiences so important to social interaction.

We turn to TV and computers to satisfy our social urges, and our society continues to regress in its social skills. I hire many people and interview many more, and after a number of years, one of the main conclusions that I came up with is this: The younger generation would rather do almost anything but make the effort to connect or socialize or call on new people. So, we are becoming an isolationist society. Is that what causes so many social problems, such as substance abuse, mental illness, and violent tendencies?

Reality TV, extremist shows, and sensationalism gain the highest ratings in the entertainment business. Because we are not experiencing enough in real life, we must turn to virtual realities and TV shows to satisfy our human needs. I cannot help but see the nuclear family option as diminishing in society. Many turn to charities, nonprofits, churches, and government agencies for support. The family unit is broken in many areas — with an over 50% divorce rate in this country, the courts are clogged with divorce cases. We find ourselves in a big social dilemma.

Another fast-growing segment is people receiving senior services. We can find one common element among the growing population of senior citizens: They are lonely. They are depressed and hungry for love, affection, and connectivity with other people. As civilized societies, how can we continue to ignore that fact? We know that due to career changes, the standard residency in one area is five years, and the average person will change their job and/or career path about eleven times in their lifetime.

So, how do we keep traditions alive, nourish values, hold on to interdependent relationships, and satisfy our social hunger to love and be loved?

We can accomplish this by building social networks and encouraging connections within our families and our local community. For example, make it a point in your life to carve out time to stay in touch with family and friends. You can host events, plan gatherings, or travel to see loved ones. Keep in mind what others value most; send them birthday notes, be an active listener, and be considerate of their feelings. Be there for their celebrations and stand by them in the tough times. Create memories of their experiences to share and savor. Teach these values to your children, and expect them to take part in family events. "It takes a village to raise a child," right?

On the community level, promote activities that connect people with each other. These could be affinity groups, service clubs, or social programs. Church and sports groups are a major way that people stay interconnected. Strong community and civic organizations play a big role in senior services and activities. Many community groups have formed to address the needs of local homeless people. Pet programs create a bond of love, especially for disabled groups and seniors. Community arts and performance programs support the creative sides of citizens and help make for a better local society.

I believe one of the things we lack is community initiatives to bring people together to talk and debate these hot-button issues. This is needed to counteract organized religions and political groups that push ideologies that are no longer tolerated by well-educated people. Now, don't get me wrong; I'll be the first to tell you that there is room for religion and values and the teaching of good people beyond family, but it is not enough. We must beware of the radicalization of people, which is gaining momentum and successfully penetrating young minds. I watched the city of Aleppo, Syria, fall because of radical organizations that have preyed on young minds who were trying to fulfill a need to belong and satisfy their social yearnings.

As I stated at the beginning of the chapter, there is an intrinsic need for you to build a network of friends to visit and socialize with. The older you get, the more important this becomes. I was at a relative's wedding a few years back, and the only person who showed up from the groom's side was a single friend. What is wrong with that picture? Everything! The groom was not sharing the most important day of his life with the people in his life. This suggests that he is a lonely person, who has either lost touch with family and friends, or they live far away. Long-lasting loving relationships are an essential social need. The word "fellowship" is somewhat of an unknown to the young millennial generation.

Stephen Covey, in his book *The Seven Habits of Highly Successful People*, said that to live, to learn, to love, and to leave a legacy are some of the most important habits one must develop. In this context, love and social connections go hand in hand. While you are building your financial success plan, you must not ignore the need to build and maintain a network of social connections.

It takes significant time, effort, and commitment on a continuing basis to keep a solid relationship going. Though it might feel tiring, and at times inconvenient, the rewards are worth it. Connectivity and social skills are some of the most important elements of success. Charlie Tremendous Jones said, "Your success in the future will be determined by the people you meet and the books you read."

Isolation has detrimental long-term effects, as I discussed before; not only on individuals, but on society as a whole. We must deal with this issue early on, especially in our young children. Social skills are survival skills for human beings, and are not optional. Developing social skills at an early age is critical to emotional intelligence. One example is making sure that your children shake hands and say hello and goodbye to visitors. This may seem a trivial thing, but it is a way for them to connect with others. In my own family, when I host parties and social functions, I have my children introduce themselves and help offer drinks to people and refill their glasses. That simple action has paid massive dividends — it taught my children about the importance of social connections and put them in place to watch people during healthy interactions. Family gatherings were a big part of their upbringing, and I know in their current occupations it gives them an edge. They learned to integrate social and business functions and practiced how to communicate effectively and interact with people from all walks of life.

The Ocean of Emotions

We all voyage through an ocean of emotions during our lives, the most basic being the desire to love and to be loved. Intimate relationships, family, and friendship all have elements of love and caring, though of different types. Developing and maintaining love requires effort, but it is an enjoyable kind of work. That said, selfish people will always have a problem with maintaining relationships because they focus on themselves and do not like to go out of their way for others. Love requires sacrifice, and if you're not willing to sacrifice, you're not going to get very far in the realm of relationships.

All types of close relationships with elements of love require commitment and trust, and if you live your life without trusting or being afraid to trust, it will be hard for you to be very happy. Every once in awhile, you are going to get hurt — it's just a part of relationship. But, as we explored earlier, the alternative of isolation is a sad way to live, to say the least.

Romance and Reality

Most of our intimate relationships will move through the following stages: romance, reality, and possibly on to rejection. Sometimes we experience aspects of all three stages simultaneously in a single relationship.

In the **romance** stage, we are twitterpated. We are experiencing all kinds of exciting emotions and wonderful feelings. However, sooner or later, we see the person for who they are — a person with flaws. Do not forget they are seeing the same thing in you. **Reality** is who they truly are; not what you are seeing in them through the rose-colored glasses of romance. Eventually, some relationships start to cool down in this stage, especially when the subject is out of sight and, therefore, not in the other partner's heart or mind as much. Dealing with that reality is never easy.

Be clear on the objective and desired outcome of each relationship. Most people today are in search of instant gratification, and they expect the other person to continue in their original romantic image. These are unrealistic expectations. Just like you and me, our partners, relatives, and friends have their own unique character flaws. They age, they change, they get sick, and they make mistakes. Be patient and keep loving them; acceptance is a virtue you'll do well to embrace.

The key is to stay in the romance and reality stages and avoid having the relationship move toward the rejection stage. Relationships remain vibrant when excitement and wonderful feelings return regularly, even if they are not always present. When reality hits, it takes personal strength and commitment to sustain the relationship. Don't forget the promises you made previously to love and stay with the other person. Of course, it takes two to tango, and you don't have control over the other person's reactions and choices.

There are two laws in nature we cannot ignore: the law of gravity and the law of decay. An old friend said to me that life is like a roll of toilet paper — the older you get, the faster it goes. While that is funny, it makes a whole lot of practical sense. Who knows, maybe that is God's way of letting us know that life is not going to last forever. When I was young, I could not wait until I hit my next birthday to get older. Today, I realize the people who told me life is short were absolutely correct, and I wish I would have listened to them more carefully.

Rejection

Rejection is something we all must face over the lifetime of our close relationships. In the **rejection** stage, when reality does not meet expectations, the value of promises made disappears easily. The romantic picture of that person disappears, and working on the relationship is no longer an attractive option. Control is often part of what is stressing the relationship, and loss of control is part of the fight. Constant fighting takes place and deception follows, and slowly, love disappears. Indifference and the death of the relationship follow, sometimes for clear and obvious reasons, and sometimes for reasons that neither person can ever quite figure out. I suppose that is part of the mystery of life.

Due to economic pressures, career demands, and the avalanche of information we handle in our daily lives, people have less and less tolerance and patience for each other. Many seem to walk away from relationships easily and without remorse, as if they are in relationships without commitment or responsibility. Our country has one of the highest divorce rates, and many single parents are raising children alone. Traditional social norms expect both parents to do the work of raising children, but the traditional family is changing, along with social networks that provide support. Social boundaries are moving rapidly, and new models have not yet become well-established. This combination is causing a social breakdown. Our ancestors did not experience the new lifestyles we are facing today. Broken promises place more responsibility on single parents, placing additional stress on boomerang children moving between separated parents, or back into the grandparents' home. When grandparents must raise the third generation, this often puts extreme pressure on the older head (or heads) of the household.

The best navigation through the sea of emotions is to avoid reaching the place of rejection, whenever possible. If you pay close attention, you can observe when relationships start to turn sour. Take some action to get your emotions and the relationship back on course. Sometimes people can work together to find ways to reclaim the romance and reality stages of their relationship. At other times they may need professional help through counseling. If both continue to value their relationship, there is usually a way to put it back on good footing.

Relationships are the process through which you shape your life. Remember that you are molded by what you experience, what you think about frequently, and the total sum of the conversations and relationships you have had. This collection of things, including the learning and knowledge you acquire through them, makes the whole you. Living life fully requires us to cherish those relationships, build on them, and create memorable moments in the time we have left on this earth, because these are the elements of being human.

Choosing Your Social Network Wisely

As we have no choice about what family we are born into and have limited choice about our relatives, it becomes very important to choose social networks wisely. Since our relationships have such an important role in molding us into who we are, we must choose them selectively. One way to do this is by using our natural ability to sense people's energies. In the universe around us, there is a constant flow of negative and positive energy. Science has proven the existence of these energies through such measurable things as electromagnetic fields and heat signatures.

Let me ask you this: When you walk into certain places or meet certain people, do you feel their energy, whether it has a negative quality or positive quality? Most of us would answer the question with a resounding "yes." Every person and place hold and projects a certain kind of energy. The geometry, chemistry, and physics of energy are all around us if we just look closely enough. If everyone has a different energy about them, then who are the people and things we need to surround ourselves with in order to achieve our best? If you surround yourself with people who hold negative energy, who tend to be pessimistic, never believing they will amount to anything, you will likely be dragged down with them. However, if you surround yourself with people who are full of positive energy, who are constantly improving themselves, both personally and professionally, you will likely be motivated to do the same. We need to carefully identify who those positive people are and spend more time with them in synergistic ways to keep moving forward.

Over the past few decades, especially with the advancement of technology and introduction of social media, many of us thought that we could be independent and work in our own private spaces, away from everyone. As a result, many of us saw our social skills diminish as we interacted mostly with machines, limiting the use of our senses and communication. This experience of becoming increasingly disconnected causes separation anxiety, stress, and social awkwardness. The time has come to step away from the electronic screens, identify the people with whom you want to grow in relationships in real life, and ultimately reach a higher level of contentment as you work in an interdependent way together.

We all seek relationships that produce true mental and emotional happiness. You can think about the energy flows in relationships in terms of bank accounts. Relationships are like a bank account; if you want to draw good energy, time, and commitment *from* them, you need to make deposits and keep the relationships going by investing the same things *into* them. For example, I have certain relatives whom I never hear from unless they want something. After years of doing my part by staying in touch and including them in family functions, I decided I am better off without them. They have overdrawn their account. If you have people around you who are constantly making withdrawals without any deposits in return, it might be time to think about releasing that relationship as well.

Part of evolving in relationships is adding value to and drawing value from other people. You should ask yourself this: Who can I add value to today, which adds value to me? This leads you to identify people who fulfill the purpose and contribute to the desired outcome of what you do daily, weekly, and monthly. You can prioritize and plan weekly, and the collective work of these weeks takes you to the desired results. In the long run, the collective results of your weekly and yearly relationship outcomes will create the social networks that form the basis of a meaningful life.

CHAPTER SIX

SEA 6: Navigating the Storms of Life

A s we sail through the Seven Seas of Life, we must expect to face storms from time to time. These storms may build up slowly over weeks or months, or may come on suddenly when we least expect them. Storms in our lives can be personal, such as divorce or loss of a loved one, related to business problems, or due to financial difficulties such as unexpected medical bills or large investment losses. When things get hard, people often quit on their dreams and settle for the path of least resistance — but that is also the road that leads to nowhere. If you're ready to work hard and push past the resistance, let's talk about how you're going to get there.

As I reflect back on all the obstacles I had to overcome, I recall a few big ones. These had a significant impact on me and the person I became. The decisions I made later in life were influenced by these events and how I overcame those challenges. Three "storms of life" stand out in particular. When I was four years old, I had to overcome the death of my father at age 35 from a heart attack. Later, as a teenager, I faced making the big decision to leave my old country and come to the U.S to go to college. I chose to take this big step despite not speaking the language and having only $300 in my pocket. The third big storm was the premature birth of my daughter.

The first big shock I had in the U.S. was running out of money shortly after arriving and the humbling experience of borrowing money to live. Finding my first job as a parking attendant was also sobering. Leaving friends, family, and my first love behind was a totally devastating experience, as well as struggling to make ends meet. For me, having a burning desire to move forward and get back to my former level of economic comfort was a major driving force for success. Coming from an environment of plenty with total abundance, and then facing basic survival challenges and barely getting by was a huge lesson. Thank God it did not take me long to improve my situation. By holding multiple jobs while going to college, it took only two years of struggle to reach a better economic level.

At age twenty-one, I decided to start a family after courting a beautiful young lady. We got married shortly before my last semester in college. I was holding down three jobs and carrying a full course load. I entered the financial services industry the week after I graduated, and shortly after, I took a commission-generating job, which brought new opportunities and challenges my way. I am glad I did. Working for a salary was not going to get me what I wanted and where I wanted to be. I only had $500 to my name and plenty of credit card debt at that time. This was a big storm of change that was made even more difficult by becoming new parents a few years later.

The new world of commission-generated income set me on a course of personal and professional development. I had to overcome the volatility in my income, so I become very consistent in my client calls and follow-up. I feared failure in keeping up with my goals of increasing my weekly income. But, my persistence and consistency paid off, and I went from $350 a week to $1,980 a week in just two years. At the end of those two years, I was promoted to Sales Manager.

Life brings us all trials and obstacles that I liken to the crashing of the waves in the ocean. The waves come with regularity; some small and some big. Many of us try to manage it, while some go to a dark place and try to hide. That dark place is called fear. But what if we learned to embrace the waves, allowing them to crash over us and accepting them as a part of life? What if we faced our fears?

The Fear is Real

What prevents us from doing things? Fear. Fear is real, whether it is a fear of failure, fear of rejection, or fear of the unknown. If you let it, it will take over and put you out of the game. Fear of success is also problematic to some people, thinking they need to be humble, in a hidden place, and that showing their wealth is not a good idea. Success and accomplishments often will be attacked, no matter what. You need to find ways to overcome your fears and move ahead.

Knowledge is important in handling fears, but organized knowledge put into action is what gives you the power to create new possibilities and provides the energy that drives your engine and keeps your ship going. Advancing your specialized knowledge and increasing your work value, as discussed in an earlier chapter, is one example of organized knowledge put into action. Although that is a big undertaking, it will propel you to climb the economic ladder. If you ask me, it is worth it. This gives you greater self-confidence and is a valuable tool against fear.

When you have achieved success, recognize that others will be jealous and will covet your Money Tree, which will be our metaphor for financial success. Do not fall into fear of these people, but instead, set your sights on taking care of your financial situation. Growing your Money Tree is a big part of your life, so what about the weeds, bugs, winds, and climate? All the above will slow the growth of your tree, and you must be aware of and ready to deal with them when they occur. You must be prepared to deal with the obstacles swiftly so they do not slow your growth. One day, you will stand in front of your Money Tree, proud of yourself and your accomplishments. Not only will it bring you joy to stand underneath its branches, but it will provide shade and prosperity for generations to come. Together you will enjoy an abundant harvest, both for your own benefit and to share with others.

There are ways to protect yourself against the weeds in the garden and the people out there trying to get to what you built without paying the price of success and stealing other people's assets. The court is also full of those cases. Do not be vulnerable. Instead, avoid worrying by seeking the help of professionals in making sure you protect and build a wall around your estate, making it crash-proof.

There are situations that come to us that are beyond our control and leave us hopeless, dejected, and sometimes furious. Mother Nature's fury, divine acts, crimes, and wars are things we just have to understand as being part of the mystery of life; we cannot figure out why they happen to us.

The biggest wave in my life yet was the premature birth of my second child. Having to live in a hospital for three months of my wife's difficult pregnancy was incredibly stressful. Then, we contended with the birth of a two-pound daughter. Seeing her fight for her life every day, while it was agonizing, also gave me encouragement and resolve. She survived and did great, which I attribute to her dedicated, loving mother, a healthy environment, and being provided with anything she needed or wanted. In her early days, we were lucky to have a nurse who cared for her, loved her, and stayed daily by her side until she gained weight and momentum in life. She grew into a strong and healthy young woman, graduating from college with an emphasis on urban planning and sustainability. She became a productive member of society and dedicated herself to working with nonprofit charities. This is an example of how the actions of another person toward a child can, in future years, help alter the child's destiny and support her to make a difference in the world.

My wife took the challenge of raising the children in a traditional model. I worried about being a good provider, taking care of finances, and furthering my career. She kept up with our children's needs, discipline, and daily problems. It worked well for us, and we are very proud of our three great children.

Some years later, I survived a bad auto accident due to a careless individual dropping a ladder from his vehicle on the busy freeway in front of me. This experience made me decide that recording and creating memories for my family is a critical part of my legacy. Over the years, I lost relatives and good friends, mostly due to accidents. I came to the conclusion that you need to pursue your passions and not wait until later because tomorrow is never guaranteed.

I acknowledge that many things and events can totally be out of your control. Being someone who contends with challenges and faces fears, you should not give up when the waves come and crash all over you and your ship. Keep your hand on the helm, stand strong, and never let go. The key is to have a plan. You can make adjustments, change deadlines, replace the players in the game, and redefine priorities.

There is safety for your Money Tree that comes from creating multiple sources of income. Many years ago, I left a credit manager position that was paying a salary and entered into the world of commission jobs. At the time, I did not understand the value or the potential in creating multiple sources of revenue. I didn't understand how those sources could multiply over the years. One of the main factors that contributed to my wealth building was being able to earn money from multiple and variable compensation plans that have many drivers of income.

Deal with fear and follow the system on how to manage and control problems. You are the chief executive of your life, and every day you need to make decisions on relationships inside and outside your business. You should promote some, demote others, and fire the bad ones — both plans and people. Build your plans based on what you want. Some people will jump on this ship of yours, and some will jump off. That's fine. Some will pass on the ride and leave you. You cannot control how people will react, and many people seldom change. It is your life, your ship, and your journey.

Going back to the canvas of your life, both you and I know that we are here to serve an important purpose, fulfill a unique role, and make a difference in other peoples' lives. You have been given a set of skills and gifts to use to complete the bigger picture. Most of the time, you just can't see the impact yet.

Life has many mysteries and a grander plan than you might imagine. Have you ever wondered what happens when you sleep; where you go, and what you see? Your state of ordinary consciousness leaves you, and you become part of the state of unconsciousness, and perhaps enter the super-conscious state. Time has no restraint, and gravity is out the window. Is it a picture of what is to come in the afterlife? To perform at higher levels, you must be aware of a higher state of being — a higher energy and spiritual level. The God factor, if you will. Can we tap into this world and see a glimpse of it so we can get more clarity and understanding? Many say yes. The universe is vast and complex, and our understanding of it is limited by our five senses. We need to think about tapping into the expanded states and mysteries of the universe to have more clarity and understanding of our purpose.

Stop Worrying and Start Living

Worrying is the psychological treadmill that goes nowhere; in fact, it drains your energy and robs you of your peace of mind. Many people lose sleep worrying about a problem or a person, unable to shake their troublesome thoughts. Trying to think of something else doesn't work, and their minds keep returning to the problem. They explore options but can't find solutions, and their fears start to consume them.

Worries are a sustained form of fear, mostly things that will not materialize in your life. Idle chat prevents a lot of people from reaching their potential and steals from the enjoyment of life. I cannot tell you how difficult it is to stop worrying. It took a very long time and many disciplines to be able to control my worries. Festering is not healthy either, and facing trouble and worries requires a systematic approach we have addressed in previous chapters. Avoiding the problems but still worrying about them is *not* the solution.

So, how do you deal with it, and what do you do to minimize the impact of worrying about things that are unlikely to materialize in your life?

Recently I read a book called *Principles* by Ray Dalio. He takes an excellent scientific approach to worrying about problems. Ray explores options and solutions outside his own perspective, and talks to at least three people who are knowledgeable about the subject. Then, he writes down his thoughts and what he has learned from these people.

Worrying is one of the struggles I have dealt with for my entire life. My wife calls me the "festerer." We all have a Ferris wheel in our brains; our thoughts are racing around and around in a circle. The question is, how do you stop it?

Unfortunately, you cannot stop the Ferris wheel, but you *can* minimize the effect it has on you. While dealing with the worries and anxieties of life, ask yourself the following questions:

What is the worst outcome that could happen?

Can I live with it? Or will it kill me?

From that point onward, you have a choice. You can decide to do everything in your power to try to alleviate the perceived problem, or you can keep worrying. I will tell you that the price you will pay if you continue to worry is far greater than actually doing something about it.

The following are some basic techniques you can use in analyzing your worries:

1. Get all the relevant facts and players and make a list with the impact of each and the best outcome you desire.

2. Write all possible solutions down, and choose the best outcome. Sometimes the first solution you think of is not the best; you must look at all possible solutions from different perspectives.

3. Design an action plan based on the best possible solution and set deadlines, listing names of people and types of help they can provide to carry out the solution.

4. Stay focused on the action plan, keep busy with needed activities, and you will notice the worrying about the problem will subside slowly.

5. Always learn the lesson and write down what you learned from this experience, regardless of the outcome. Keep records and review them yearly. This will help you learn and profit from the lesson and bounce back.

The above is easy to say, but hard to put into practice. It's not how many times you are going to face adversity and fall, but rather how fast you can bounce back that matters.

Life in the Fast Lane

As much as we may hope it will be, life is not all that simple. We live in a highly technological era with smart devices, computers, social media, and artificial intelligence all around us. Robotics and electronic communications and transactions are the way of the future. We live in a world that has become so fast-paced that it demands continuous learning from us, usually requiring more working hours to stay abreast of developments.

How do we become better adapted while surviving the constant changes and the speed with which they are coming at us? In my lifetime, as I mentioned before, I have gone from watching a box-like television in black and white with three channels to watching a large, high-definition flat-screen television with vivid, true colors and endless channels to choose from. How does one make sense of all this progress and keep up with it in order to evolve?

Dealing with rapid change and the challenges it brings requires a plan. It calls for you to evolve with the changing times. Your efforts to overcome setbacks, obstacles and adversity along the journey often need to change. Much like your blueprint to financial success, strategies are required, and a written plan is essential. The beginning point is re-discovering yourself and what you value most, what you are passionate about. You will re-explore your inner dimensions and reorganize how you can live a full, successful life with a great legacy that you can leave behind. This evolution will involve the thoughts you create, the actions you live out, and the decisions you make.

Keep in mind your answers to the following questions: What makes people happy, and what makes people secure? I am sure that money is a critical part of both (among many other things, of course). Creating and protecting wealth is one of the major components of personal happiness. You can't expect someone else, such as the government, to take care of this for you. Today, the U.S. government has become a giant spending machine with no end in sight. The system is so complex that despite being among the highest taxing nations in the world, the U.S. must borrow additional funds to feed this bureaucratic country. Therefore, you cannot count on the government to take care of your future needs. This should be a wake-up call for us all. You can only count on yourself; the days where a worker could count on employer pension plans are over. Many of the baby boomers will be turning to their children for help. In other words, they will have too much of their lifetime left after the money they have saved is gone, and they must turn to relatives for support.

Your strategic plan will help you handle all this rapid change. There are multiple ways to protect yourself and your businesses. Read the books, work on the plans, and seek the professionals to help you protect your estate. Seek reliable and experienced financial consultants; I caution you about the amateurs in the arena. Some of the people around you, who all have different opinions, may not wish you well. Some may gloat about what is going wrong in your life, while others will be happy to see you succeed. Choose the people you spend time with wisely.

Spending time with the people you love and care about is one of the best legacies you can leave behind. This provides a lifetime of memories for you to enjoy and your loved ones to remember you by. For example, I remember very little from my grandparents on my father's side, but have so many memories that shaped my life from my grandmother on my mother's side. The stories, the prayers, the meals she fixed me, her love for me, the discipline she instilled in me, how she bargained and shopped and ran a big household, how she made sure her children were always in touch and set expectations that framed my entire life.

Life in the fast lane may cause casualties in your relationships. I have had a few regrets, and the one I will carry with me to my grave is my wish that I had spent more time with my loved ones and told them how much I loved them. Mistakes I made, relationships I did not keep up with — the biggest hurt is to lose people you love from your life. Witnessing diseases take over relatives as they aged and the demise of good people, coupled with being away from my mother when she passed away, hardened my spirit and made me realize that life may not give us many chances. To me, that means seize the day. Take full advantage of every opportunity life offers, especially to be with those close to you and share love.

Among the legacies I plan to leave, one of the most important is creating memories for my children and grandchildren, and providing for anything they need or might need in the future. I am intent upon giving them a head start that I did not have myself. One hundred years from now, my name will become another name recorded in human history. Deep inside of me, I know that the world for my children and grandchildren should be a better place because of what I created for them.

We are small cogs in the big wheel of life. The diary of the future will record the value that we contributed to our families, communities, and the world. What do you want to be remembered for, and for how long?

A Tale of Two Possibilities

Picture yourself standing in a long line of people on a cold day. You are hungry, your stomach is empty, and you're waiting for a handout or a meal in a public park. Your feet are hurting from moving all day, and you are wearing someone else's shoes, which do not fit your feet. The clothes you are wearing smell of someone else's cheap cologne and old, stale cigarettes. After getting some leftover food at a food bank, you may or may not be able to find somewhere to sleep that night at the local shelter.

Who else is in that line? Homeless people who might be addicted to drugs, have behavioral health issues, jobless, or just down on their luck. Along with these unfortunate people, you may very well end up sleeping on a piece of cardboard on the side of the street, next to a family that is also homeless, with young children and a cold, dirty dog.

In contrast, picture yourself at home in a warm place, beautifully decorated with your personal belongings and collectibles. It is reflecting love, security, and peace. You are surrounded by loved ones, looking at them as they are eating, playing, watching television, or spending time on their smart devices. You're sipping wine and having dessert after having eaten a delicious home-cooked meal, enjoying your fireplace, and reflecting on the flames of life's possibilities.

These scenarios contrast, but those are two very real (and common) images of what life could look like. There are consequences to the decisions we make, and life does not cater to what we need, but rather what we earn through our efforts. To illustrate my belief in this, I kept a reminder beside my computer. I held on to a mouse pad for thirty years until it was totally worn out because of a message it had written on it. On the mouse pad was a picture of the Serengeti Desert in Africa during sunrise, a lion, and a herd of gazelle with a quote by Christopher McDougall which said, "Every morning in Africa, a gazelle wakes up; it knows it must outrun the fastest lion or it will be killed. Every morning in Africa, a lion wakes up. It knows it must run faster than the slowest gazelle, or it will starve. It doesn't matter whether you're the lion or a gazelle — when the sun comes up, you'd better be running."

The moral of this story is that the circle of life goes on, and it serves the enterprising and the strong. Failure and success are two opposite possibilities, much like good and evil. You have the responsibility to embrace success, and you potentially have what it takes to be successful: the goals, skills, discipline, and willpower. Claim those as your own and hit the ground running.

You can take the helm over many possibilities in your life. During my years of corporate life, I encountered many bosses. Some I liked, some I did not like; some liked me, and some did not like me. I could not help that, but how I reacted to these circumstances is what mattered. Some of my bosses could crush my opportunity for the next promotion. At times, I wanted to quit and give up because the normal business day to day challenges felt overwhelming. I adopted the golden rule that follows: *Never, never, never let one person or one business deal stand between you and the success you are after*. That lesson came early in my career. A client's check bounced due to insufficient funds, and I had already begun spending the money. After that experience, I resolved to never let it happen again.

I avoided such problems in several ways. Of utmost importance was staying on the merit side of the business, paying close attention to the numbers and income statistics. I watched closely for evidence of achieving business objectives and disregarded empty talk and hollow promises from others. I kept my distance from others, staying respectful of their contributions but not becoming dependent on any one person in driving for results. Keeping work value in mind, I constantly improved my skills and expertise so I would remain a valuable asset in the business. I stayed away from the political side and avoided currying favors. To further avoid depending on one person or business deal, I created many opportunities in business and formed a large social and business network.

I learned early on that people do things for their own reasons — not yours. The lesson here is do not hang your ladder of success on the wrong wall or behind only one person. They can leave the organization or fall down in their promises without notice. Over many years of corporate life, I had to deal with seeing many people fail in the commission business, and I had to overcome difficult corporate politics and bureaucracy. Being a gatekeeper to many peoples' careers in financial services was helpful for me despite the challenges and high degree of failure I observed. Today I am proud that I hired, developed, and trained many people to be leaders in their field. In return for this assistance, I enjoyed seeing them have great lifestyles, raise families who had financial abundance, and climb the corporate and business success ladders.

Dealing with Vultures

As we see in the story of the lion and the gazelle, nature and life have no mercy. The game of life is played in nature as well as with people, but we have evolved to play more sophisticated games. You must now ask yourself, who are the vultures when it comes to your life? I assure you they are out there, waiting for you to get either mentally or physically weak enough in order to make their move on you and what you have. The older I become, the more clearly I see them around.

They come in all kinds of shapes, some in sheep's clothing, pretending to be your friend while waiting for an opportunity to take advantage, just as a wolf would using a sheep's hide to get close to the herd. As we become more vulnerable, more predators show up, and it will be of utmost importance to watch out for them. Each one of us is given 20 to 30 years on average to set up the financial foundations of our lives. After this, our earning capacity usually declines. You must build a fortress around that foundation to protect not only your own building, but the ones of the generations to come. I often say to many of my financial advisors and representatives that they have one good shot at setting up their clients' retirement. In most situations, there is no redo, and there is no part two, so they must do it right the first time.

Having a good support network is a real asset in setting up your financial foundation. Society in the United States is increasingly nomadic and transient in nature; people go to where the good jobs are, and very few stay put. The geographical security that used to come from putting down roots and staying in the same place is long gone. There are a lot of benefits to staying and building a support network of friends, family, and service providers. They not only offer us a sense of community, but also help us strengthen our fortress. We see that Eastern societies value family more than Western ones, and it is common for those raised in Eastern societies to make personal sacrifices for family members.

Nothing even close to that can be found in Western societies, based on my observation. So, which is better? A collective or an individualistic society? Nobody really knows; each has its own advantages and disadvantages that would appeal to different personal preferences. But how is all this related to dealing with vultures? As we become older and the vultures begin circling, we need a protective wall around us consisting of our network of people and whatever structure we have built for support.

Having spent over 35 years in the financial industry, I have seen some terrible vulture behavior that cannot be ignored. Among the most common, most egregious issues include preying on people, especially the elderly, identity theft, white-collar fraud, and undue pressure put on the weak and mentally challenged. However, these bad behaviors are not only practiced by those in power. These behaviors are also engaged in by employees. Conning your employer is quickly becoming a new trend. There are employees who prey on the system and try to blackmail employers; they make this their profession and hide their tracks after they're done. There are cheaters and liars all around, and they are all types of vultures.

You will encounter vultures along the journey to build your financial foundation and protect your wealth as you age. There are many ways to stay alert to con-men and predators, whether within your work and friendship circles, internet scammers, business associates, or false telephone solicitors. Senior citizen associations and internet scam detection services offer lots of good information. Your best safeguard against vultures, however, is your own "fraud alert" system, which keeps you aware of people's attempts to take advantage.

Emerging from the Storms

For all the challenges and setbacks in my family's life, there were just as many victories and wins. We arrived at many pleasant destinations during our journey. I earned plenty of recognition and powerful positions, which included multiple awards and promotions. By this point in my life, the ego has been very satisfied. Now, my next challenge is to "kill the ego," a phrase used in spiritual and psychological practices that means going beyond satisfying personal desires and goals.

Many of these career and economic successes contributed to affording me the opportunity to live a balanced life, fulfill my three major goals discussed in previous chapters, and travel around the world in luxury and style. As I have emerged from the storms of life and reached an island of security and prosperity, I have the capability to make major contributions to the wellbeing of others and to the world. This is another important part of your legacy: what you leave behind and will be remembered for.

Most important to me are contributing time and money to three major causes I am passionate about. They are:

1. Helping the elderly and the aging

2. Clean water projects around the world

3. Providing for humanitarian causes and medical missions

On a local level, I enjoy being involved in community civic and charitable organizations.

In between the storms, we will encounter calm waters and sunny days for us to enjoy. As our voyage across the Seas of Life nears its conclusion, we can experience these enjoyable conditions for longer and longer periods of time.

CHAPTER SEVEN

SEA 7: Growing and Protecting Wealth

The Money Tree

As you sail the Seven Seas of Life, you will pass many islands, and some of them will be covered with trees. But the one you are looking for is the island that grows Money Trees — your Paradise Island. The Money Tree is what we will use as a metaphor for growing and protecting wealth.

Next to oxygen, money is one of the most important things in our lives. With that in mind, let me ask you this: what is important about money to you? If financial stability were a tree you planted and watered, how would you grow your money tree?

It begins with good seed in fertile ground, the seed being our philosophy about money. We are all stewards of money, and money flows *through* us. Some of us are wise with investments and make it grow, while others are merely a conduit through which it flows fast. None of us are going to take money with us after we're gone, so while we are on this earth, we should be good stewards of it. If you are a good money manager, you will attract more money to yourself in your lifetime, and that money can be put to good use.

Most people would agree that they desire to build and accumulate wealth. Of course, this isn't all life is about, but I'm sure you understand by this point in the book that it is a vital part. In building your wealth, start with the desire to have what you want when you want it, whatever *that* is. Maybe you want a beautiful place to live in and call home, a car you love, exotic places to visit, delicious food and wine, or the company of the people you love.

So, how do we measure wealth? By reputation, possessions, net worth, the good relationships we have, or how healthy we are? Personally, I think all the above are measures of wealth. However, for the purpose of this chapter, I would like to focus on net worth — specifically, your *personal* net worth and how to build it.

The Uses of Money

In my opinion, the most important use of money is to provide yourself and your loved ones with a good life. The second is to allow yourself to achieve your personal and professional goals. The third is buying yourself time and financial freedom. Discipline to manage money is like building a strong trunk that will support all three; a trunk that can withstand the winds that come your way in your future. Some say that if you cannot save money in your lifetime, you cannot cultivate the seed of greatness that everyone has within, thus stunting the growth of their money tree. I believe this with all my heart. I have seen many people who did not save and have lived a life of poverty, envy, and regret. So, I ask you again, what is important about money to you? Generally, how a person spends money is a good indicator of where his or her passions lie.

Growing your money tree begins with designing a financial plan that works for you. While this might seem straightforward, the difficulty lies in developing the *discipline* to create wealth. First, accumulating that wealth and growing it to the next level may require that you embrace delayed gratification. There will always be a reason to spend the money now.

Moderation is the key to financial success while you are building your wealth and growing your money tree. Many businesses tempt you to spend now for instant gratification. Think about sales — when you see something on sale that you don't necessarily need, you think to yourself, *But I'm saving money buying it now. If I buy it another time, it won't be on sale.* It's simply a tactic that appeases our desire for instant gratification.

Any time you have the urge to spend more *now*, ask yourself the questions below:

What happens if the paycheck stops?

What happens when all the money is gone?

These questions should shape the way you spend money. Do you need it? Or do you just *want* it? Don't get me wrong; you can still enjoy life and have the pleasures of spending while you save and avoid truly unnecessary expenditures that adversely affect your plan. However, we must have the future in mind as we think about spending and saving.

So, why exactly am I advising about growing your money, and what credentials do I have in this field?

In a nutshell, I have dedicated my entire professional career of over 35 years to studying and practicing financial sciences. I hold Chartered Financial Consultant and Chartered Life Underwriters designations, as well as an Insurance Fellow designation. These advanced designations in the financial and insurance fields show that I have taken additional professional development and specialization, along with many licenses in the securities and insurance areas. I became a self-made millionaire applying the concepts you'll read in this book, and my hope is to help you become more prosperous and financially secure as you read.

Essentials of Wealth

The essentials of wealth include your personal savings, your home, your personal possessions, and your car. Next comes protecting these items by making sure you have a plan to cover them in the event of loss or accident. Insurance is a critical part of wealth building, yet most of the time, it is ignored. Many people are under-insured or not insured at all. You want to have insurance policies that cover the replacement value of your personal possessions.

Protecting your wealth requires coming up with financial goals for the long term. Spend some time brainstorming about what is most important, and come up with a number that represents the net worth that you need to achieve in order to gain, maintain, and enjoy your desired lifestyle. I'll admit, that's definitely a difficult number to figure out. Take your time and really think about what you want and need. Once you have the number in mind, the real question is this: What will it take to actually get there?

At this stage, it would be helpful to seek the guidance of a financial advisor to assist you in coming up with a financial plan and formula to achieve it. A financial advisor has the ability to test the financial formula against your objectives to see if it will accomplish your goals within a realistic time frame and numbers.

The process of building and protecting wealth will take multiple steps:

1. Discipline to save money over a long period of time and not touch it, allowing it to accumulate and grow.

2. A certain amount of money to be saved and invested weekly/monthly from your income or a percentage of total take-home pay.

3. Financial products to put the money in, which could be a savings account, money market account, life policy, retirement account, annuities, stocks, or bonds. Seek those that offer compound interest.

4. Monitor your return on any interest or dividends you gain on these accounts.

5. Invest in tax-favored (meaning tax-deferred or tax-free) financial products when possible. Many of these tax-favored plans can be found in retirement accounts, such as 401k plans.

Now, it will take time to let the magic of compound interest and long-term planning work for you. Compound interest means that the interest money earned on your financial products is not taken out, but rolled over into the principal to add even more interest growth. Patience is going to be key! Even when temptation arises, you must discipline yourself that this money is never to be used when you have the urge to spend. This money should be allocated for your long-term financial success. The key is to create future cash flow from sources other than your wages or work. Watch the net worth grow and enjoy the fruit of your labor.

If you live in the United States and you understand our tax system, you probably know that you should have a small business to take advantage of all the tax breaks our system affords. If you are employed, you can take advantage of what an employer can offer in tax-favored programs.

The purpose of these financial products and accounts is to cover future needs and desires, such as retirement income, college funding, and purchases, such as a cruise after you retire. If you are clear on the objectives and purposes of your money, you will gain the willpower to use discipline and avoid cashing out early.

Now that you have built an estate from your assets and attained a healthy net worth, what is next?

Take Care of Debt

I like to think of one's money like a ship sailing the seas, where we are given a certain number of years to reach our destination. There are only two ways to ensure that the ship moves forward: adding more sails to catch the wind blowing from multiple directions, and making sure you are fixing any holes that would cause it to sink. So, while you are working hard on adding sails, you need to also mind the leaks. Many small leaks here and there will sink your ship fairly quickly. These types of leaks include paying for your lifestyle, debt, interest, and fees. The biggest leak of all, however, is taxes.

Taxes are an obvious leak for many. If your earnings are always taxed, you will have significantly less money in the future. If you can save money that is not taxed, is tax-deferred, or tax-free, you will have substantially more money in the future. Debt is the silent killer of your Money Tree and a significant leak in your ship. Consumer debt from credit cards or financed purchases is a true killer; I liken this debt to an infestation of bugs that can destroy your Money Tree. If you don't take care of the bugs, they will bring your progress and growth to a halt before you know it. Thankfully, there is a way to live a debt-free life and be released from the bondage of exorbitant fees and interest. If you have debt, it is critically important to include a **debt reduction goal** in your financial plan.

We live in a debt-oriented society here in the United States, which is also why many people stick to a job they hate and are never able to get out of the cobweb of credit card debt. If you find yourself in this category, here are some solutions to consider.

1. **Organize and Prioritize Debts:** Account for all your debt, organize it by the highest interest rate, and make it a point to pay the accounts on which you owe the least amount of money first, followed by the ones you owe the most on. That way, you're eliminating the number of outstanding debts you have.

2. **Pay as Much as You Can:** Avoid making minimum payments on credit cards, and pay extra every opportunity you get to close out your debt faster. For many years, I carried multiple credit card balances, and it took me seven long years to pay them off. However, if I had made a plan and tackled these accounts with the intention of closing them out one by one, it could have been a much faster process.

3. I can assure you that the balance of your savings and investment will grow at a high speed if you no longer have debt to slow you down. Get that burden of debt off your back as you march toward your goal.

4. **Diversify:** Over the years, you can protect your wealth accumulation by having a solid financial plan with a focus on diversification. In the last 35 years, I watched the market go up and down. I watched three crashes: the crash of 1987, the crash of the bond market in 2000, and the mother of all disasters (before COVID-19), the crash of 2008. Many businesses and individuals were practically wiped out. They went to sleep as millionaires and woke up as paupers. Personally, I experienced declines in my real estate values and equity in my homes. However, throughout these crashes, two areas stayed constant: my cash and insurance accounts. In a low-interest era, they held their values. This is the beauty of diversifying your investments.

5. **Go Slow:** When it comes to your future financial security, you should never fall for get-rich-quick schemes. Slow and steady progress wins the race in this arena, I assure you from personal experience. For those who are behind in meeting their financial goals, you will need to consult a financial professional to help you with an asset allocation strategy. This can help diversify your portfolio to take advantage of products to help you grow the money you currently have.

6. Keep Saving: It is not what you make, but what you keep that really matters. An average person in the United States earns in excess of $1 million in his or her lifetime. The question is, how much of it will he or she *spend,* and how much of it will he or she *keep*? For instance, if you are earning $50,000 a year on average for thirty years, you have earned a total of $1,500,000. To replace your income when the paychecks stop would take a minimum of $37,500 a year. So, how much must be put aside during your younger years in order to maintain your lifestyle by the time you become unable or unwilling to work? At a 5% capitalization rate, you will need a minimum of $750,000. That is significant capital to save if you are not used to saving money on a regular basis.

Think about how much you have made in the last ten years, and how much of it you have kept. If you have only held on to a fraction of it, you need to work harder on increasing the amount you save.

Managing and Tracking Your Wealth

Imagine that you have three boxes in a room: one blue, one green, and one yellow. I will give you a piece of paper, and you are to write what you own on them and put them in the boxes following these rules:

1. **The blue box is your legacy:** WHAT you want to leave behind and to whom.

2. The green box is your income: MONEY that you will use during your and your spouse or significant other's lifetime.

3. The yellow box is your business: ITS assets and its value.

Now, create an inventory on a balance sheet where you list everything you *own* on one side and everything you *owe* on the other side. This is an asset and liability list that takes account of your financial picture. These are the things you will be writing on the balls given to you. Once you have them all written down, I want you to put them in the appropriate box — legacy, income, or business. Once you finish this exercise, I guarantee you will feel better. You'll have much more clarity about your financial situation. This is like looking into a financial mirror; you may or may not like what you see. Regardless, this is a real starting point, and life becomes easier when you know your score and you are keeping count. Above all, you'll now be very organized in your head on what your estate is and how you want to manage it going forward.

You may ask, "What should I put in each box?" The blue legacy box should include things like your home, life insurance, securities (stocks, bonds, investments, commodities), money, valuables, real estate, art, jewels, and personal items. The green income box should include things like your pensions, retirement assets, 401k, money, deferred comp annuities, and income products, including money you will use in your lifetime. The yellow box is for your business assets and products, including business real estate and the business' "going concern," which is the value of your business.

How does this make wealth management easier? For example, if you have life insurance and you put it in the blue box, you will give yourself the freedom to spend more of what is in your green income box.

Over the years, I have seen enough to know that most of us will experience what I like to call a "Big Bang Event." This is an unforeseen circumstance that will require a lot of money, help, and resources from family and friends. It can come close to the end of your life or at any stage throughout. Generally speaking, these events will suction a lot of money over a short period of time, and you better be ready. For example, developing severe Alzheimer's disease that requires care around the clock can run $10,000 a month. It's imperative to be prepared for this kind of occurrence in your estate plan.

The Formula for Winning

The Formula for Winning in growing and protecting wealth can be summarized as follows:

1. Discipline to save over a long period of time.

2. Reasonable return on your money.

3. Tax-favored benefits while in the saving phase (to take advantage of current tax laws and help accumulate savings faster).

What is our most powerful asset in wealth-building? Some of us think our greatest asset is our home, bank account, household items, or our car. But the truth is, our greatest asset is our **income-earning ability**. This is taking our skillset, time, and effort into the market-place in exchange for either a paycheck or directly paid money. These represent our value to the marketplace. When looking to save more, we must ask ourselves, is it possible to increase our value and thus raise our hourly rate? Each of us starts somewhere, but we do not need to stay there. The key to increasing our income-earning ability is to increase the value we have to offer in the marketplace.

Increasing your work value was covered in a previous chapter. Just to summarize, you can increase your value in the market place in these ways:

1. Increase knowledge and professional education.

2. Acquire new skills.

3. Work on current skills and liabilities by making your strongest attributes stronger and limiting weaknesses.

4. Obtain specialized knowledge.

5. Take calculated risks when making career moves.

Estate Planning Made Easy

You will need a plan for the estate you're creating to grow and protect your wealth. This plan should include wills, trusts, estate taxation, and inheritance tax. Who is going to manage those when the time comes? I strongly advise you to seek an estate planning attorney to execute this plan and a competent CPA to advise you on the best tax strategies. You'll also need a good insurance agent and a financial advisor you like and trust. Keep in mind they should be the best in their arena, not just mediocre professionals. There's a lot of skin in the game when it comes to estate planning, and you need to know you have somebody you can trust completely. If debt management is part of the plan, you need a private banker with a very strong bank whose resources are on your side. Debt management can include how you plan to pay off debts you may have taken on, such as business or real estate loans.

Don't assume that I have all the answers, but I am choosing to share with you what worked for me. When I started building my estate, I had absolutely nothing.

I started on my estate planning on a whim when I got home after a long night working as a parking lot attendant. Remember, that is when I was at the bottom of the economic scale, working just to survive with only $300 to my name. I began taking $1 from every $3 I brought home and putting it toward long-term saving because I had quickly learned that planning for my future was up to me and no one else. It took me about 15 years to put the first million together, using the plan I shared with you earlier. Once I reached the first million, it became quicker and easier to grow, and the rest is history.

Now, before you think I just got lucky, let me tell you something: I worked hard for what I have, plain and simple. I did not invent a product, I did not become a CEO or a celebrity, I did not take a business to the market to sell it, and I did not inherit money. I was able to build my net worth with hard work, specialized knowledge, and operating on the principle that I am the captain of my ship. Best of all, I raised three children and they finished their studies and graduated without any debt. All three are doing well, are self-reliant, gainfully employed, and looking at bright futures. They have all proudly told me they want to build their wealth on their own.

Each child had a college fund, savings, and vehicles that were paid for. I can tell you without hesitation that I take immense pleasure in creating a head start plan for each grandchild. Over the years, I have supported my mom and my brothers and dedicated a lot of my time and money to charitable organizations such as Rotary and others. Today, I am passionate about giving financial support to humanitarian, clean water, and senior services projects. I feel the best part about my estate plan is the ability it provides me to give generously and make a significant impact on people's lives.

My green box was designed to support both our current and *future* lifestyle.

Do you like what you're reading? Go to work on your personal financial inventory now. It does not matter where you start, as long as you do not finish in the same place. There's no better time than the present, right?

Protect Your Estate Plan

Even the best estate plan can crash and burn if it is not protected. You've spent significant time and effort putting the pieces into play to build and accumulate wealth; now, it's time to think about how to protect it.

What are the essential pieces of protection?

1. Adequate home, car, and liability insurance to cover replacement value and lawsuits.

2. Excellent health and disability coverage for medical expenses and income protection if you are unable to work.

3. Life insurance to replace your economic value for your family.

4. Error and omission policy if you are a licensed professional.

5. Health directives and a Durable Power of Attorney.

6. Business insurance if you own a business.

7. Trusts can play a big role, including limited liability holding companies (you are advised to consult legal and tax professionals on how best to insure yourself).

Protecting, accumulating, and distributing wealth will require many hours of dedicated study and planning. After all, it is your money, and you want to manage it well. It's best to continue the plan you've developed, rather than taking out money and having to keep restarting over and over again. Don't miss out on one of the most valuable elements of financial planning — the time you need for your money to grow through accumulation and compounding interest.

There are three directions you can take when it comes to estate planning:

1. Make no plans and have your heirs suffer the tax consequences. Without plans, your estate is subject to Federal or State taxes within nine months of your death. The government and the IRS will demand tax payments based on the value of your estate. In essence, they become your partners in the estate you spent your entire life building.

2. Make a formal plan on your own and self-operate it. I can tell you to a certain degree that if it does work and grows, you are undoubtedly going to need the services of professionals later.

3. Seek the help of estate planning professionals and a team of legal, financial, and tax advisors to help you formulate your plan.

Estate planning is for everyone, not just the ultra-rich who need it most. It requires deliberate and intensive strategizing. Seek the guidance of competent estate planning professionals that can help you clarify, organize, and put a plan together. I promise it is well worth your time and money.

You're in Charge

Building wealth is a philosophy I live by. It is an obligation every person should undertake, no matter what position or income level they currently have. Saving and accumulating for you and your loved ones is your responsibility while you are playing your role here on earth.

Wealth building is important. You are either working on your wealth plan or someone else's plan, and other people generally do not keep your best interests in mind. Narrow your goals to a specific amount of net worth (money) you want to have by a certain time, and be clear on what you are willing to give in order to achieve that goal: time, effort, new learning, new skills, or putting your existing skills to work. Make it simple and keep in mind that you could lose it all without insuring it: your life, health, ability to work, and what you own. Shifting the risk to an insurance company is a very good idea.

The investment world is large and confusing. Invest with experts who possess a proven track record of success in managing people's wealth. Invest with experts and firms with good financial ratings.

The reason *why* you want to build wealth is one of the most critical factors you have to deal with. Once you identify the reasons why, you are well on your way. But always remember: You are the one in charge.

Most of us are conditioned since childhood to play a part in someone else's plan. It could be a plan designed by our parents, employers, spouses, or a church leader. It is perfectly OK to be part of such a plan while you are a student, still learning. But eventually, you'll need to launch into your own plan, based on your own goals, desires, and philosophy. To make this plan happen, you'll need a hefty dose of self-confidence to make the changes in your own life.

Taking charge of your life takes courage and discipline, and standing for your beliefs is essential to living a happy life. On your journey, you will encounter discouragement and setbacks. Even though we all experience the waves of life crashing over us, we have the choice to persevere and not quit in fear of getting bowled over. Many people live, work, and raise families with very little accomplishments and die with unfulfilled dreams. Don't fall victim to the fear of stepping out on your own.

If you are part of someone else's plan, they generally see you as part of the *cost* and not the plan; their rewards for you are small in comparison to your value. That is why many workers do not feel satisfied with their jobs. Make yourself valuable to the marketplace, and the marketplace will reward you, because the marketplace is blind to your background, education, and looks. Your income-earning ability is your greatest asset there.

In taking charge of your legacy and wealth-building, remember there are three ways to make money, and only three:

1. You at work – the money you earn.

2. Your money at work – investments earning money for you.

3. Other people's money at work – your percent earnings as someone's partner, money manager, or advisor.

Use these three ways of making money as they apply in your life to build wealth and leave a legacy you can be proud of.

Disclaimer: I advise consumers to seek legal and tax advice from their own legal and tax advisers. They should evaluate their financial strategy annually to take into account changes in their personal situation. Financial strategies will vary with each individual, since strategies reflect an individual's current financial situation, age, future financial goals, need for liquidity, risk tolerance, etc. An individual must qualify for life insurance and long-term care insurance via underwriting, and taxes are only one of the considerations when evaluating a financial plan

CHAPTER EIGHT

You, Too, Can Design Your Life

Y ou are the captain of your ship, sailing across the Seven Seas of Life, setting your course to reach Paradise Island. This is, of course, a metaphor for designing your life to achieve financial success and personal satisfaction. Hopefully, by now, you have some guidelines for charting a course to a satisfying and secure future.

Legacy by Design

A legacy is a part of you that becomes immortal — based on what you leave behind — that can impact generations to come. This doesn't just include your assets and wealth, but also your hopes for the future and causes you believe in. To live a varied and fulfilling life is one thing, but to make a difference in a child's life is a different level of accomplishment. Many years from now, a child's life can be better because of the contributions you made during your lifetime.

By making the world a better place to live, these contributions, whether to humanitarian charities or research that improves living conditions, will help generations to come.

The legacy you leave behind is an important part of the cycle of life. What will become of your digital data after you are gone? What will happen to your pets? Most people make no plans for these types of things in their estate plan. Again, the most important legacies you will leave behind are your assets, journals, pictures, and above all, your reputation. Make plans to secure all of these things, and make sure there are people who can find them and manage them after your life has ended.

Your legacy also includes the direct impact you have on an individual's life. Today, I am the product of the contributions many people have made in my life. I am part of their legacy, and I am forever grateful for their love and forethought and the opportunities they gave me to become who I am today. I have deep gratitude to my family, to my parents who gave me a good start, and a grandmother who helped raise me after my dad died when I was four. Two of my uncles set a great business example in my life and gave me the opportunity to come to this great country. My aunt gave me love and support through my struggles.

Many others are part of my legacy. I learned a great deal from my Jesuit priest who opened my eyes to philosophy and religion. There were many lessons from my scout leaders and my school teachers. Friends, lovers, the mentors in my life, my bosses, executives, and business associates all made important contributions. I learned from the hundreds of people I hired and promoted over the years, assistants and staff who made things possible, advisors and professionals who I relied on for their expertise. I am especially thankful for my close and longtime friends and their families, my wife, who stood by me through thick and thin, my family who I love dearly, my children and my grandchildren, who bring me tremendous joy and happiness. I am their legacy, and they are mine, both those who are present now and the ones who are no longer here.

Along your life journey, many people entered and left, as with mine. You may wonder what happened to them. Like you, some of them overcame adversity and challenges. Others did not. The older you get, the more you come to recognize that we are the total sum of our decisions. You want to make decisions that enhance your legacy. Now is the time to fortify and protect your Paradise Island. Keep the maintenance going so it retains its beauty and does not become just another ruin in the history books of life. Practicing what you learned in this book will help you grow your assets and wealth to serve your family and good causes.

There will always be something new to reach for once you reach your first set of goals and dreams. Naturally, you will seek new horizons and new sets of challenging goals and priorities. This is like the captain of a ship who reaches the first destination and goes on toward new ones. It is not only the money and net worth you attain during the journey, but the character you build and skillsets you develop that matter the most. Who you become as a result of pursuing your goals gives you the ability to win life's challenges and come out triumphant against the storms you faced during your journey over the Seas of Life. I am a product of building wealth from nothing and now able to share it with my family, community, and good causes. That is precisely why I am sharing this with you. Do not wait for an inheritance or a lottery ticket or a jackpot; go to work on your plan now.

The more I look around me, the more I see this life as part of a master design, and that the brain is a conduit for a higher purpose. When you fly and start to see things from a higher elevation, buildings and mountains get smaller and smaller until everything looks like dots, all interconnected in some way. When you think about it, isn't that the way the world is meant to be? Interconnected? When you ponder the meaning of all of it, think about your legacy by design. Think about the contributions you can make to others and the world. When I remember people who helped me, every day I know they are looking down on my life, reminding me that we made a difference in this life. So, I ask you: What difference do you want to make in the lives of the people you love and care about, the causes we struggle to resolve on earth, and what kind of world do you want to leave behind?

After we are gone, most of our family members a few generations from now will not even remember our names, let alone what we have done and how we lived. Ask someone what their great-grandfather's name was, and they most likely do not know. This does not have to be true for you or me. We can change that by making sure we leave a legacy, a legacy to be remembered for generations to come. Many years from now, the difference you will make in a child's life will be a legacy. We stay connected with the departed through their memories and the impact they have on our lives. You can make a lasting impact.

Fulfilling Your Passions

One of the easy ways to discover a person's passions is to watch how they spend their time and money. You can think about these as their habits and hobbies. For example, I love estate planning, luxury cruises, film and epic movies, fine and antique art, gourmet food, and social time with friends and family. If you look at the majority of my personal spending, you will see that it goes to those areas.

Outside of these things, charity comes next among my passions — being able to share money with people who need help. For many years, I contributed to various causes and foundations. I gave the majority of my contributions to senior services, humanitarian and clean water projects.

Supporting senior services is important to me because, from my experience in the financial industry, I found that many people run out of money before they run out of time. Today it is critical to plan for a long retirement, taking into consideration that we are living longer than ever. However, many people don't make retirement plans. Money and services are needed to support the millions of baby boomers who are retiring in record numbers.

They make a serious mistake by not gearing up for retirement with a well-thought-out plan and scientific approach to figuring out what it will take to support their future lifestyle. Do not be one of them. Seek help, do your research, and design a plan. As covered in previous chapters, the plan takes careful thinking, discipline, time, and awareness of the taxation, which will set you back if you don't take it into consideration.

Fulfilling your passions involves scheduling your time well. You'll know how serious someone is about something when you look at their calendar. If you love movies, make time for movies. If you love the beach, make time for the beach. If it matters to you, put it on the calendar and make time for it. You'll be glad you did.

My love for movies started with my dad taking me to the movies when I was three, before he passed away at age 35 from a heart attack. I cherish those memories. Because going to the movies was special to me, I made it a point to regularly take my children to a nice family lunch and a movie at a local theater. Today, the next generation is also practicing the same ritual, and we find great enjoyment in it.

One of my other passions is gourmet meals and spending time with my friends sharing them. Three times a month, we make it a point to get together to either go out or dine in, gourmet style. Because I've scheduled this time on my calendar with them, I know I will have time left over for other things that are important, other passions. Having time for solitude is also important to me. Learning the art of having an inner dialogue has contributed to some of my favorite moments. Every late Friday and Saturday, I take a minimum of three hours to think, reflect, journal, and plan ahead.

Planning is a strong skill I have that has served me well over the years. If you take the time to plan your time, life becomes easier to handle. Take time to think about and write down your future projects; after all, this is where you will spend the majority of your life, right? Again, it is important to be clear on what it is that you are passionate about, and plan for it.

Creation

As I mentioned earlier, creation is the best gift given to all of us by the creator. We should build on improving the quality of our lives and the generations after us. Many people in the past have paid a dear price to make sure we have what we have today with time, effort, failing experiments, sometimes even blood. We should, while enjoying what we have, build on what we have by producing and working. Your creative intelligence can be the change needed in the future.

We are designed to achieve, create, and produce. That is where great satisfaction comes from. Most of us are born with a set of natural gifts, and we develop certain skills to be part of our strengths. Identifying those skills and strengths help you paint a better picture of your Paradise Island, knowing that you can put those skills to work.

For example, my oldest son has great public speaking skills. Today, as a part of his job, he can fill an auditorium of 300 to 500 people and captivate their attention by what he has to say. He perfected this ability over time and takes a lot of time planning for his talks; it is part of his strengths and his purpose.

The Ultimate Plan

The ultimate plan should lead you to a place in your life where you will have few regrets, many loved ones, and the freedom to spend time with them. Many of us spend our lives working and doing and not enough time enjoying what we built. To make it easier to enjoy what you built, be clear about what you want, who you like, and what you like. If you do not like something, change it. If you do not like where you are, change directions and where you spend your time. Not everyone in your life is going to agree with you or share what you are passionate about. That is OK, as long you are not asking for their charity for your purposes.

Designing the Ultimate Plan requires time, knowledge, written documents, and professional advice. If you do not want to do it yourself, hire someone who is a professional to help you. Put it all together. After all, the Ultimate Plan will require reviews, revisions, and changes. Be willing to examine it every so often. Depending on the size and the complexity of the plan, it may require a graph or an outline to make it easier for the professionals helping you to understand the big picture.

Make sure you are clear on your desired results and what brings you pleasure. Go back to the three boxes: Green for Income, Blue for Legacy, and Yellow for Business. What do you want to put in each of them? Complete a personal financial statement and inventory of all your assets prior to this exercise and remember to allocate what you want to spend during your golden years.

Filling the boxes will involve tax planning, estate planning, investment and insurance planning, and retirement planning. All of the elements must be carefully studied and organized, but what is going to drive the plan are your goals, wishes, and desires. I think with this approach, we can make legacy planning a little easier.

Do not take an amateur approach to this critical and ultimate life plan. Once you write down your goals and desires and allocate what should be in each box, make sure to capitalize on the value of any retirement benefit into an asset balance. Read the latest on estate taxation. You do not want to leave this to the government tax authority which can take half the assets, or be the victim of some judge's opinion about what happens to your estate, or be vulnerable to some distant relative who wants to claim your assets after you are gone. I say this to you knowing the lengthy case proceedings that take place in court based on what goes wrong with lousy estate planning. It is one of the main reasons families are torn apart and lifetime business partners become enemies.

How to Enjoy Your Wealth

I know some very wealthy people who have everything except the ability to understand how to enjoy their wealth and those around them. Sharing the wealth is an art form, and it is a selfless act. Hoarding everything you have, due to your upbringing or philosophy, can bring more misery than enjoyment. The question to ask yourself is: Do you like people, or do you avoid them? It takes special social intelligence and skills to like, get along with, and love others well. Think about the people who should be part of your future happiness plan. Many senior citizens today suffer from loneliness, and sooner or later, they shut off. Consider whether giving, socializing, and loving others should be part of your plan. Only you can decide if that will give you the greatest pleasure.

They say you only live once. Life is by design. Who designed yours? A higher power, God? Many of us believe that our destination is predetermined by a higher power. Others believe if something is meant to be in life, it is up to them, and they should make their own way — the "independent cowboy" way. I believe in a higher being that has given us the power to create and chart our destiny. We have the freedom of choice to chart our life course and determine how to react to what happens to us.

I do not know about you, but the older I get, the faster things move around me, and the faster the days pass. I wonder if this is only a phase and things will slow down later, or if it is a signal to get things done. I wonder about human motivation. If we find that we are going to live forever, how motivated will we be to accomplish things? Painting your life picture vividly is what happens when you explore all the colors and options available. The olden years should be golden and enjoyable as we later fade into the sunset. A life well-lived, the elders say, is when a person had a good reputation, was well respected in the community, provided for his family, and had a good family of loving children and grandchildren.

I write this book today knowing the world is full of crises, conflicts, terrorism, and war, with no end in sight. History continues to repeat itself, preventing humankind from continued progress. We should remind ourselves that if we can get stuck, we can get unstuck. We can change course and catch fresh winds in the ship's sails. We are not forced to sail in one direction at all times.

We can make changes, take a different route, and alter the plan to fit our desired results. Be true to yourself and your values, and do not shy away from serious conversations and confrontations with others, if necessary. You want to have very few regrets later, with many victories and positive memories to hold on to.

Sunset of the Journey

As the sun sets in the west and your journey toward your ideal life is completed, maybe you are thinking, "Do I have what I want, or is there another Paradise Island better than this one?" That is OK. We are built that way; it is our nature to want to have more, to be more, to create and build more. You don't have to decide on new adventures right away. Take time to enjoy your Paradise Island.

Paradise Island is a sweet spot with contentment and serenity. Know it is your own creation, and it has your personal signature. The place is beautiful, the sky is blue, and the colors are vivid. Your Money Tree is thriving and bearing fruit. You are surrounded by people you care about and love. You have anchored your ship and completed the journey. The master plan is completed. Now, you are improving and enhancing your future legacy because all your needs are mostly fulfilled. You took charge of the helm. You took care of business and built wealth to support your lifestyle during your later years. Generations to come will be better because of you and what you created.

Along the journey, you have changed lives and altered the future for others as well as yourself. Only the events in the future will determine our impact upon society and life in general. Now, you have a chance at the end to reflect back on your entire life and take an inventory. I hope you only had a few regrets along the way. Most importantly, are you surrounded by the people you love, and do you have what you want and what you care about?

In some Eastern cultures, including the one in which I was raised, they say you have lived a good life if you did something meaningful, provided for your family, and your children and grandchildren grew up to love and respect you. Your reputation is what you leave behind. If you are respected, that means a lot. Big name or small name, it does not matter as long it is yours. This is your ultimate legacy.

Your family, friends, colleagues, and network are valuable and priceless relationships you cherish. In your journey, you did your best to maintain good relationships with them and to provide for their needs. You increased your knowledge, your skills, and your value to the marketplace. You are now the chief of your own Paradise Island; the big Kahuna. Take pride in your accomplishments. The lessons learned became part of who you turned out to be today. Some of these lessons were costly, and you paid dearly for them. But, you learned many useful things and used these lessons to make course corrections in your journey.

Life is different when you do not have financial stress or pressure. These concerns now are replaced by confidence and the silent power of money — the financial security you have built over a lifetime. You did not give up or give in; you kept going and stayed the course. The closer you get to the simplest pleasures on your island, the more you will enjoy life. Keep it simple. This is your creation to enjoy in every way.

Throughout my travels, I have witnessed people who are waiting and simply existing. You look in their eyes and there is a sense of sadness, frailty, and idleness. Many seem to be waiting to die and cross over to the life after. That should never be you. You should have a zest for the simple things life has to offer, such as love and meaningful work and projects. These opportunities will continue once you have settled into life on Paradise Island, although they may be different than the ones during your career life.

Unlike most people who are on the crowded main path, you have chosen to take the path less traveled by other ships. There are many around the world who are unhappy, but they chose not to do anything about it. Not you. Deep inside you, the feeling of doing something different pulled you to take calculated risks, knowing if you want to fulfill your entire potential, you have to do things off the well-traveled path. This took you on your unique voyage across the Seven Seas of Life, a journey leading to financial security and success in life. Risky journeys can lead to unimagined outcomes. Look back at Columbus. He set sail to go to India, and he ended up finding a part of the Americas.

Vision, Precision, Strength

As this journey comes to its conclusion, I'll share one final story with you that has been very significant in my life.

Throughout my life, I have been fascinated with eagles. For many years, we lived on top of a mountain near a lake. My family was raised in a secluded, beautiful place, full of large pine trees and gorgeous views. It was a very tight-knit community. I regularly took my large dog, a white Great Pyrenees, on walks around the lake and the forest, enjoying nature. Early one misty morning, I was walking the dog on a trail adjacent to the lake shore in between giant pine trees. All of a sudden, I heard a muffled sound. The air began to shift, and six feet above my head, a giant bird with enormous wings came flying down from a bare old tree. I stopped to admire the bald eagle. It made its way through the trees and on toward the lake's crystal surface through the fog.

The majestic look of that bird up close and personal is nothing like what you see on TV or in the movies; it had a bold presence and majestic power. Its talons were visible and strong, and they looked like they were made out of Damascus steel. My eyes followed the eagle flying low above the water for about a quarter of a mile. It then dove into the water and grabbed a silver, shining trout about a foot long. The fish struggled to escape, but to no avail. As the eagle ascended back in the air, it left three ripples in the water and flew back in my direction.

It was as if time stopped at that moment. I caught myself holding my breath and slowly let it out. The eagle came toward the leafless old tree and landed on its nest on top to feed the eaglets in the nest. Such triumph is repeated in nature every day, a display of vision, precision, and strength.

Following the bald eagle's example, I wish for you the vision to see the possibilities and opportunities for success well before they become obvious, just as the eagle saw the trout beneath the lake's surface. I wish for you precision to execute your life mission with minimum setbacks, and the strength to hold on and complete the journey until the end, so you can discover meaning, success, and joy in your attainments.

Well, we have come to the end of this journey. I have enjoyed sharing with you, but most of all, I hope you have charted a course to financial freedom and have a new definition of personal success.

I wish you, my friend, the vision to see the possibilities and opportunities ahead before they are apparent to others.

The strength to hold firm at the helm and stand strong regardless of what is ahead and see it through to the end of your journey.

Safe travels. Don't forget to enjoy the journey and what you will become because of it.

Sail away, sail away.

About the Author

Roland R. Ghazal, CLU®, ChFC®, began his career in the Financial Services industry in 1984 and was the recipient of many national and industry awards over the years. He has been an accomplished financial professional and managing partner for a Fortune 100 company for several decades. Roland holds multiple financial, securities, and insurance licenses. He has been a major contributor to the success of many leaders and financial advisers in the financial services industry.

He's a self-made man, father, grandfather, and a strong advocate of financial literacy and education. Roland is multi-cultural and multi-lingual with extensive international travel experiences in many countries. He's a philanthropist on multiple fronts and a member of several professional and civic organizations.

Roland's many years of successful management experience is enhanced by his leadership in both community and professional organizations. He has a strong belief in both personal and professional development. He has earned his CLU (Chartered Life Underwriter) and his ChFC (Chartered Financial Consultant) designation from the American College; specializing in retirement and complex estate planning.

His key skill sets are strategic planning, recruiting, and both building and growing business structures.

You, too, can design your life!!

Appendix

Books that influenced me greatly include:

The Bible

Hill, N. (1937). *Think and Grow Rich.* Meriden, CT: Ralston Society

Schwartz, D. (1987). *The Magic of Thinking Big.* New York, NY: Fireside

Bettger, F. (1947). *How I Raised Myself from Failure to Success in Selling.* New York, NY: Fireside

Tolle, E. (1997).*The Power of Now.* Novato, CA: New World Library

Collins, J. (2001).*Good to Great.* New York, NY: HarperCollins

Canfield, J.; Hansen, M. (1995). *The Aladdin Factor.* New York, NY: Berkley

Collins, J.; Porras, J. (1994). *Built to Last.* New York, NY: HarperCollins

Stanley, T. (1996). *The Millionaire Next Door.* Lanham, MD: Taylor Trade Publishing

Rohn, J. (1994). *The Art of Exceptional Living.* Nightingale-Conant (Audio)

Grayling, A.C. (2019). *The History of Philosophy.* Great Britain: Viking

Clason, G. (1926).*The Richest Man in Babylon*. New York, NY: Berkley

Duhigg, C. (2012).*The Power of Habit*. New York, NY: Random House

Meadows, M. (2015). *Grit*. CreateSpace

Goss, T. (1996).*The Last Word on Power*. New York, NY: Doubleday

Goldsmith, M. (2007). *What Got You Here Will Not Get You There*. New York, NY: Hyperion

Covey, S. (1989).*The Seven Habits of Highly Effective People*. New York, NY: Simon & Schuster

Carnegie, D. (1936). *How to Win Friends and Influence People*. New York, NY: Simon & Schuster

Scott, S. (2002). *Fierce Conversations*. New York, NY: Berkley

Tracy, B. (2017). *Eat That Frog!* Oakland, CA: Berrett-Koehler Publishers, Inc.

Sifton, E. (2003). *The Serenity Prayer*. New York, NY: W.W. Norton & Company, Inc.

Marshall, R. (2000). *Surprised by Serenity*. Alliance Affinity Group

Dalio, R. (2017).*Principles*. New York, NY: Simon & Schuster

Gitomer, J. (2015).*The Sales Bible*. Hoboken, NJ: John Wiley & Sons, Inc.

Hansen, M. (1983). *Future Diary*. Newport Beach, CA: M.V. Hansen Pub. Co